LOYALTY AND ELEGANCE:
ART NOUVEAU
GOLDEN
RETRIEVERS

THIS BOOK BELONGS TO:

THIS PAGE
INTENTIONALLY
LEFT BLANK.

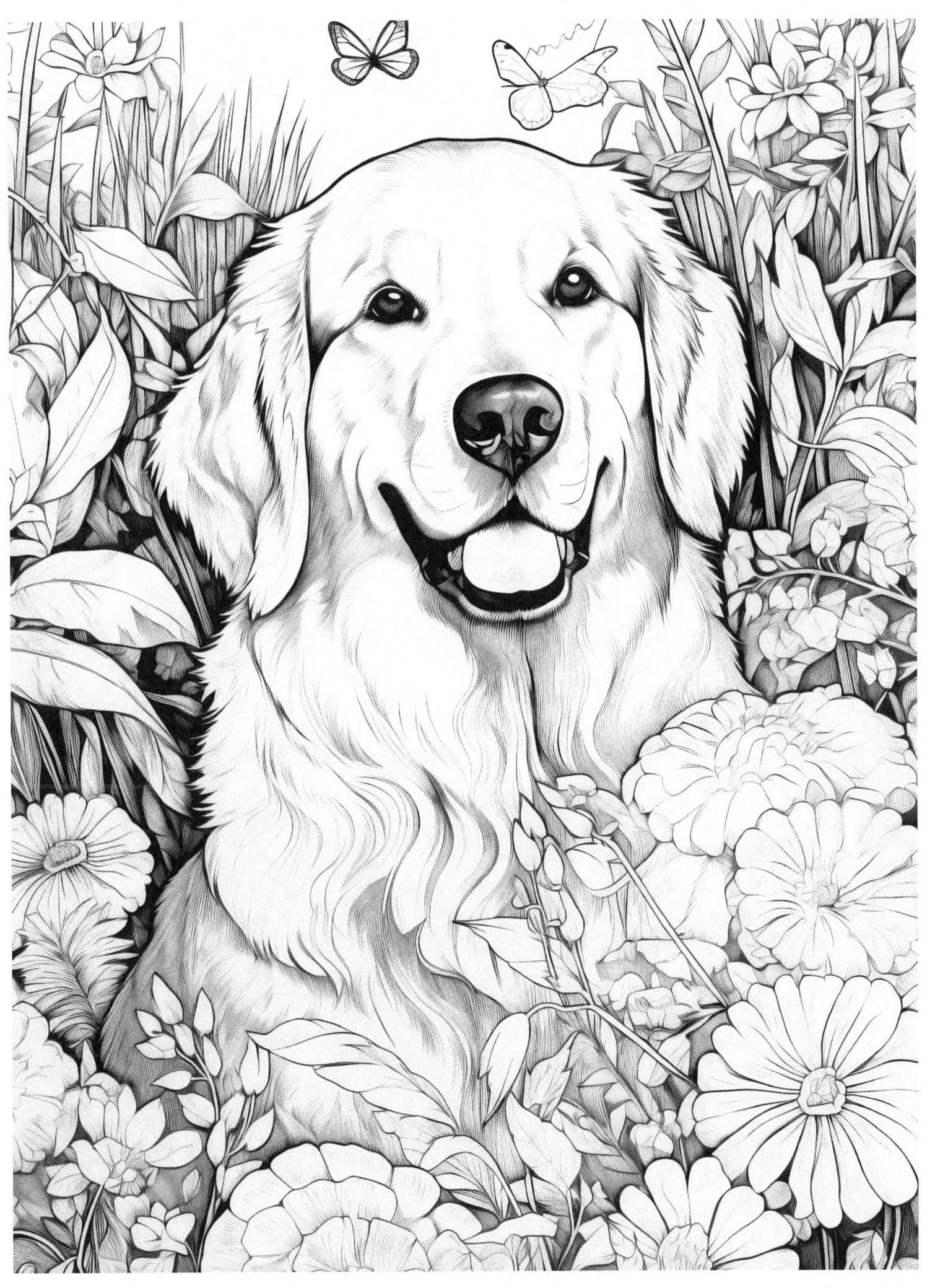

THIS PAGE
INTENTIONALLY
LEFT BLANK.

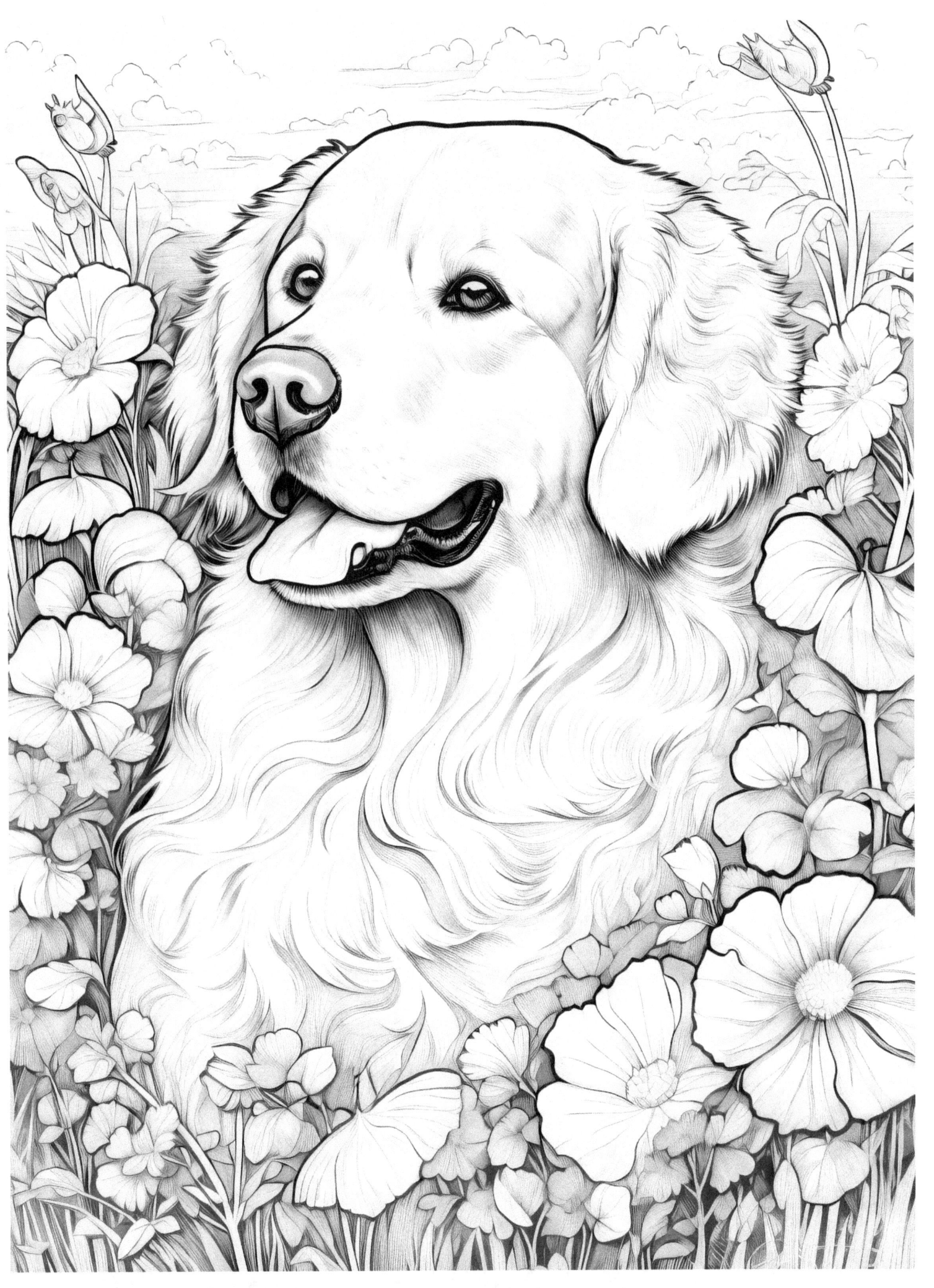

THIS PAGE
INTENTIONALLY
LEFT BLANK.

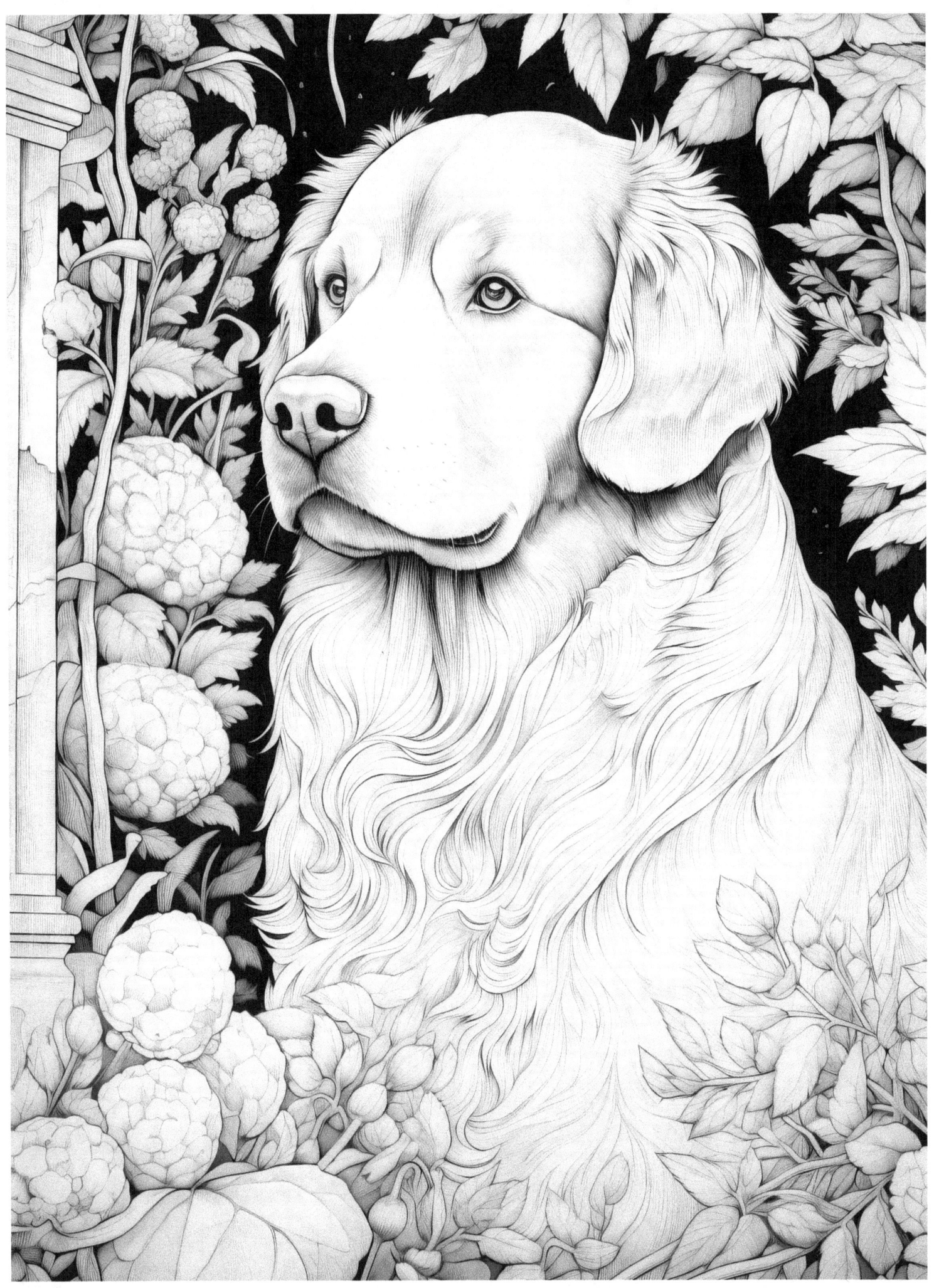

THIS PAGE
INTENTIONALLY
LEFT BLANK.

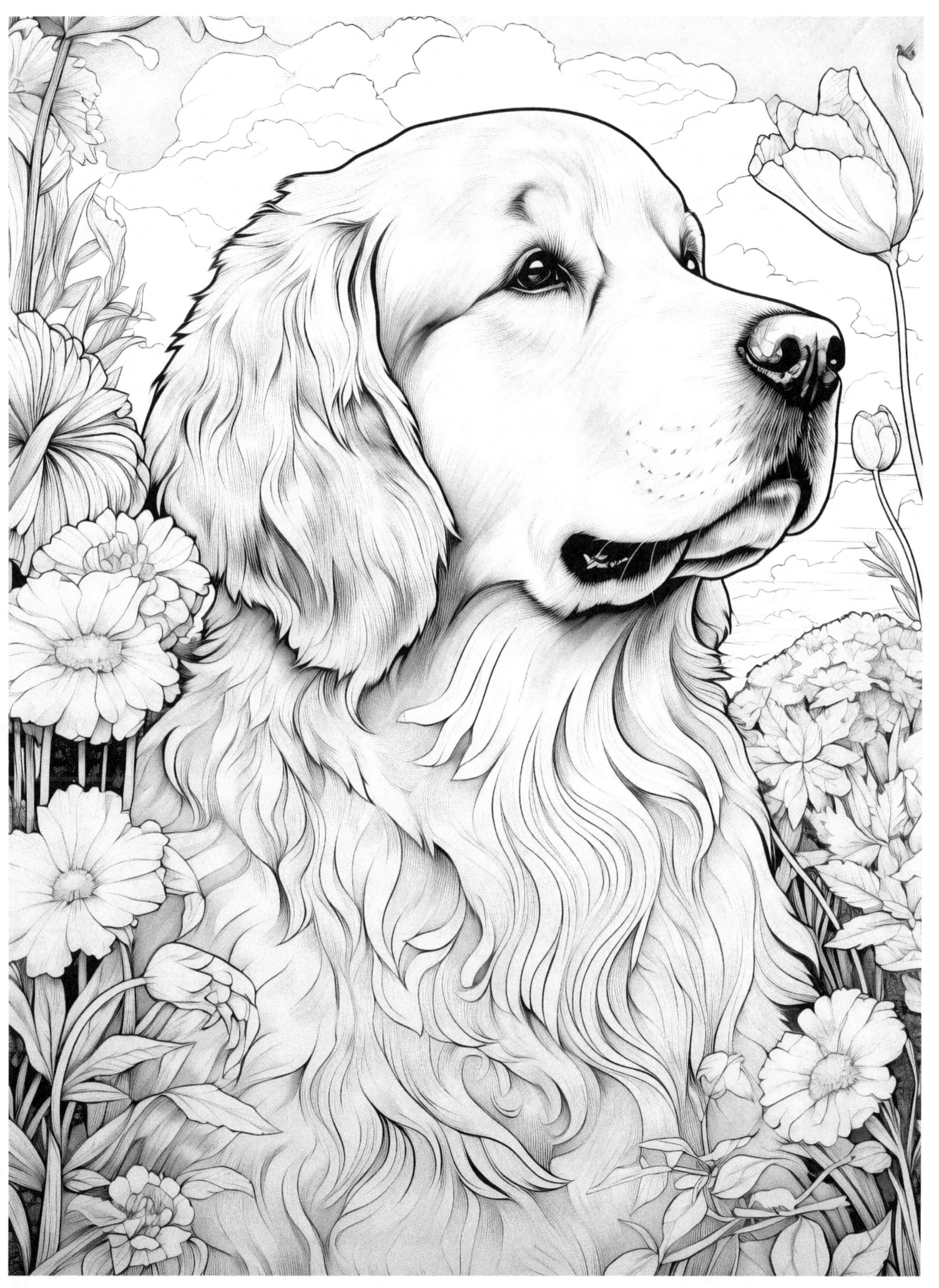

THIS PAGE
INTENTIONALLY
LEFT BLANK.

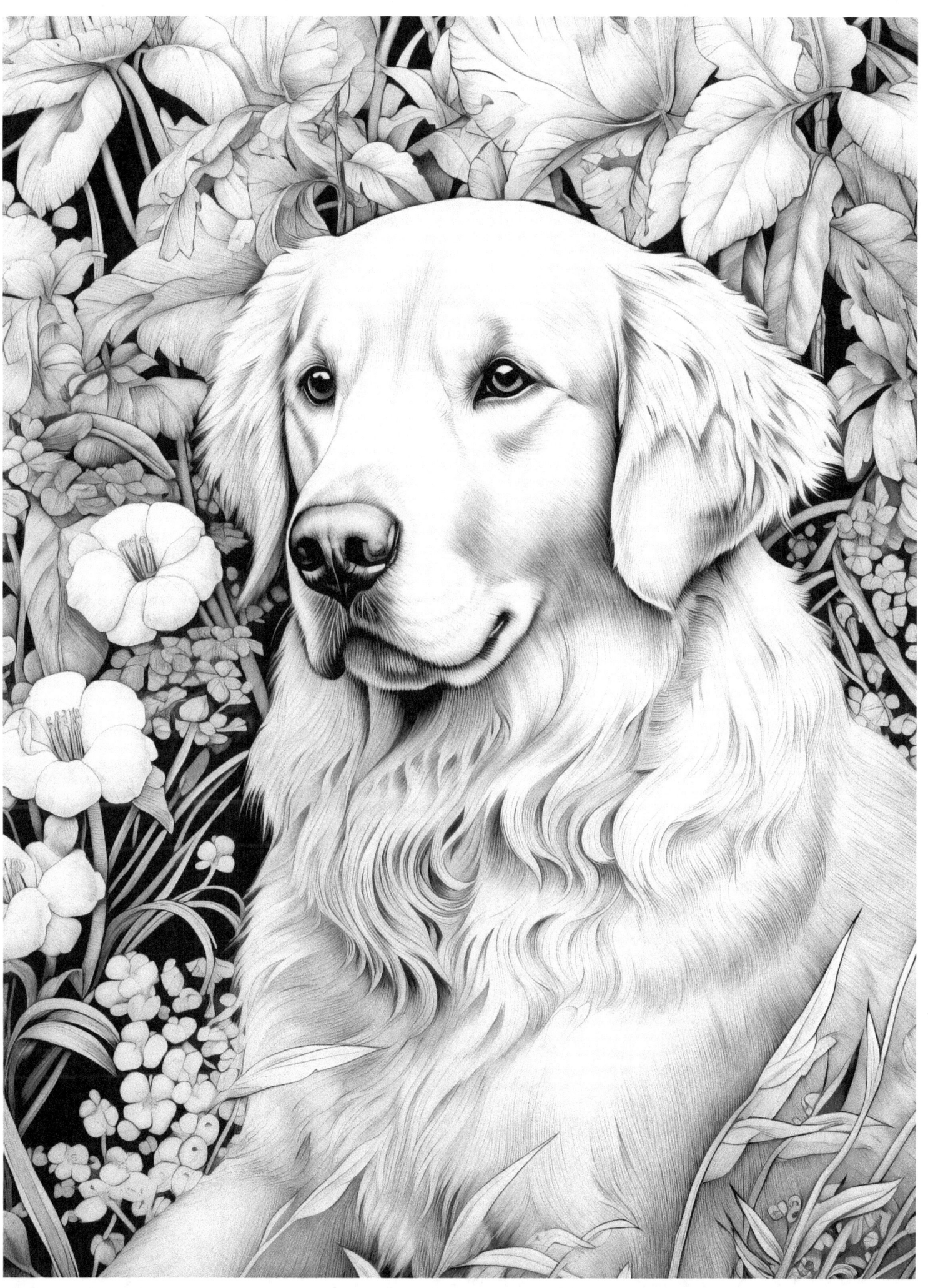

THIS PAGE INTENTIONALLY LEFT BLANK.

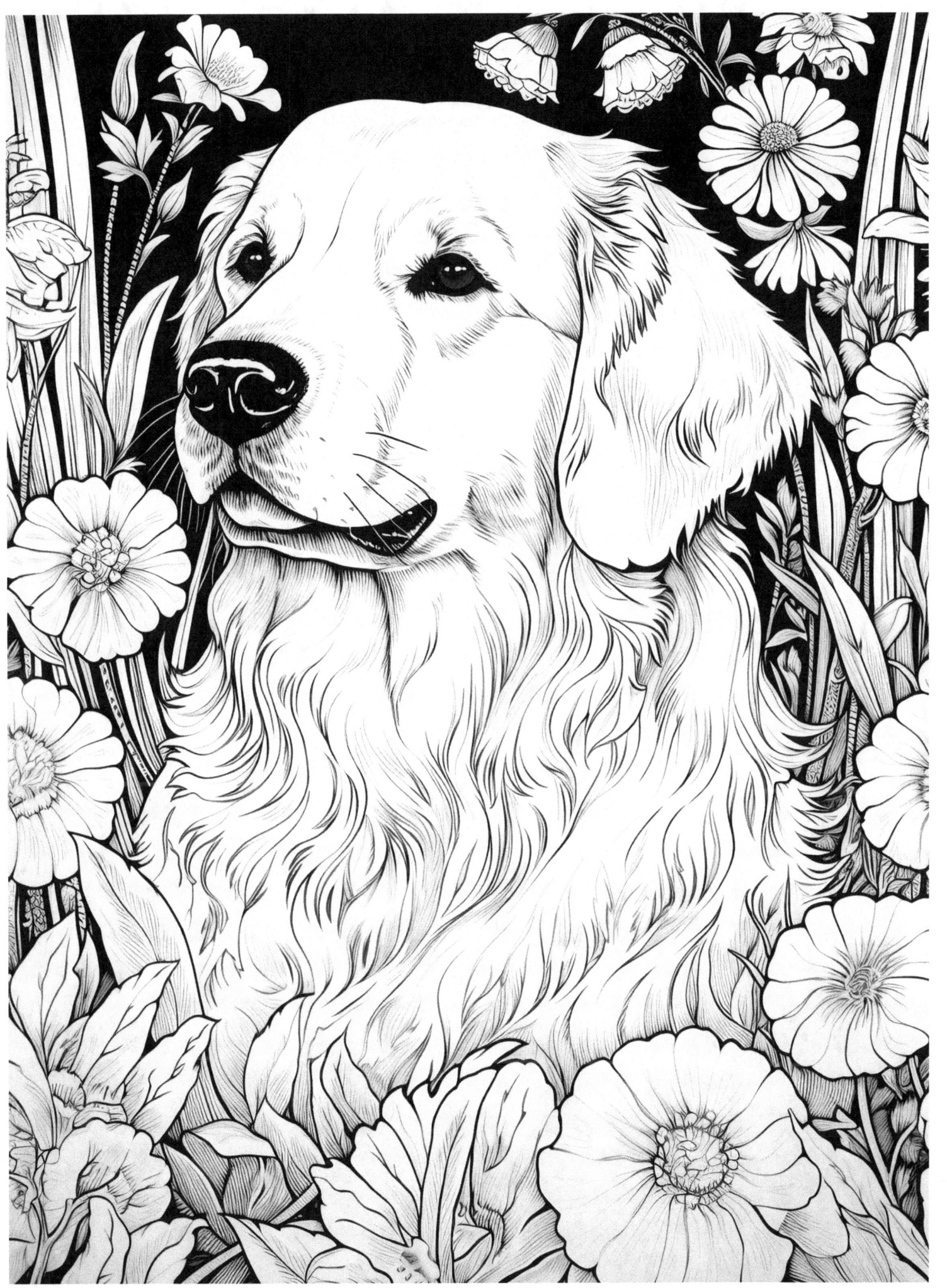

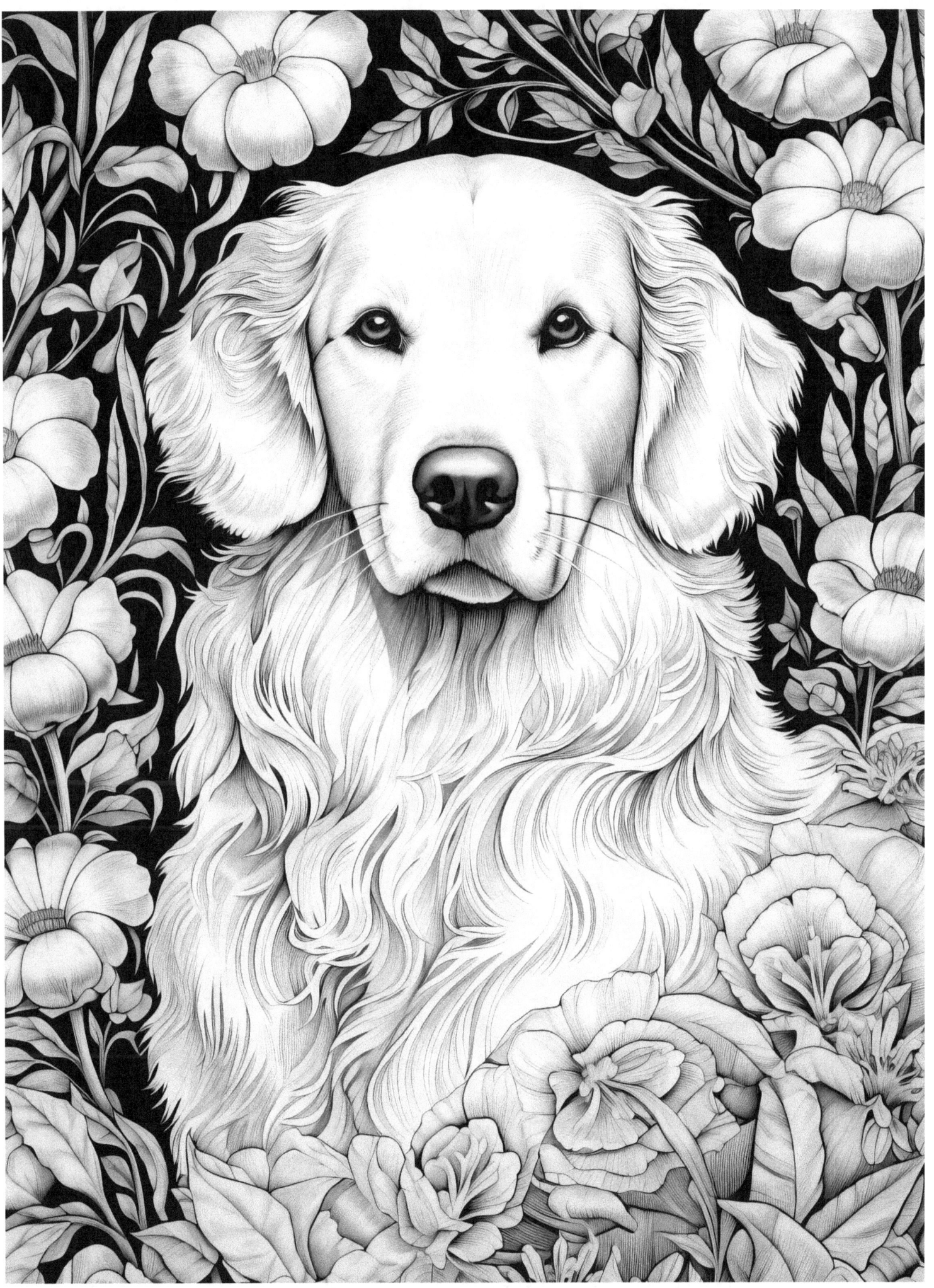

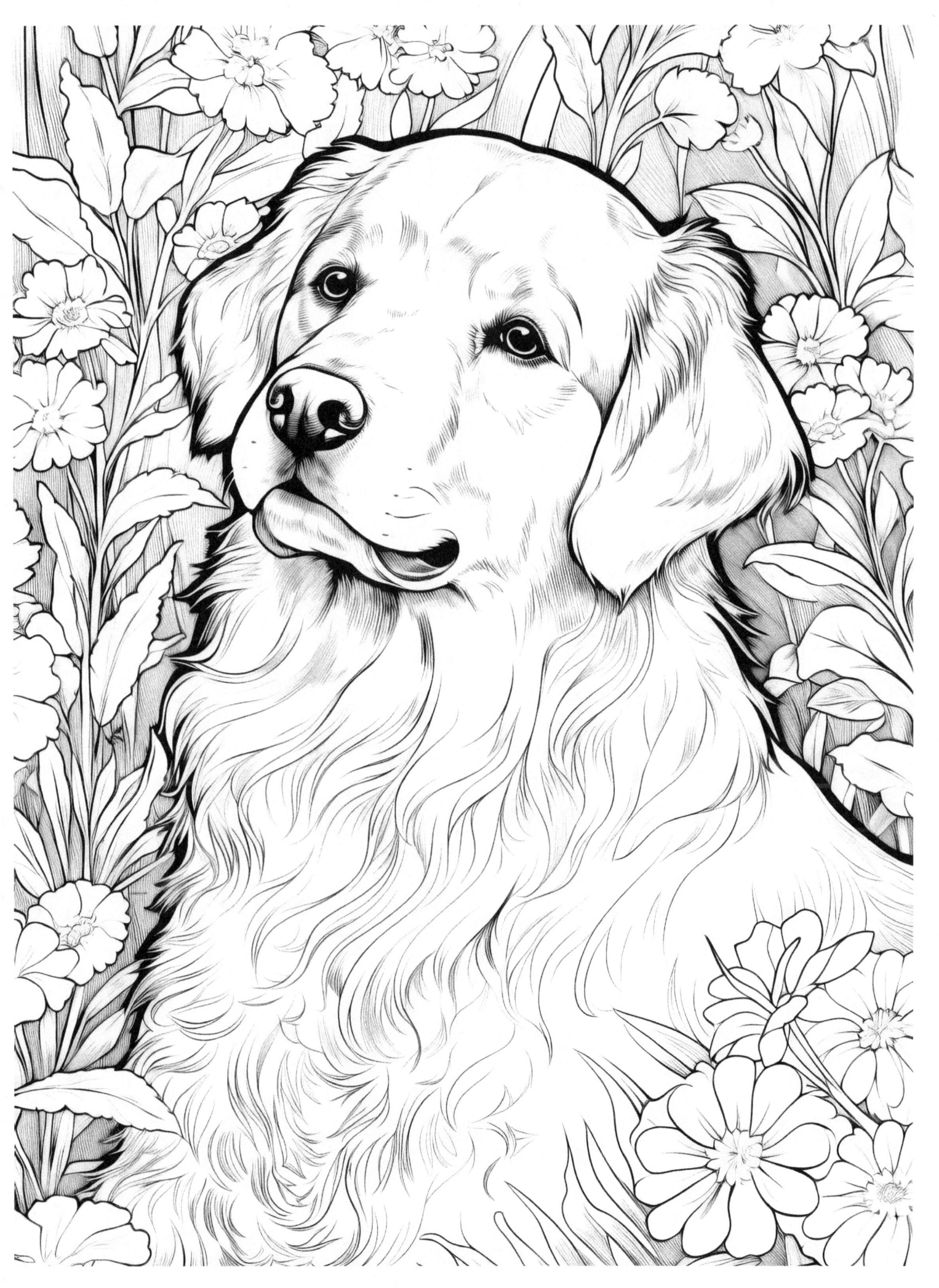

THIS PAGE
INTENTIONALLY
LEFT BLANK.

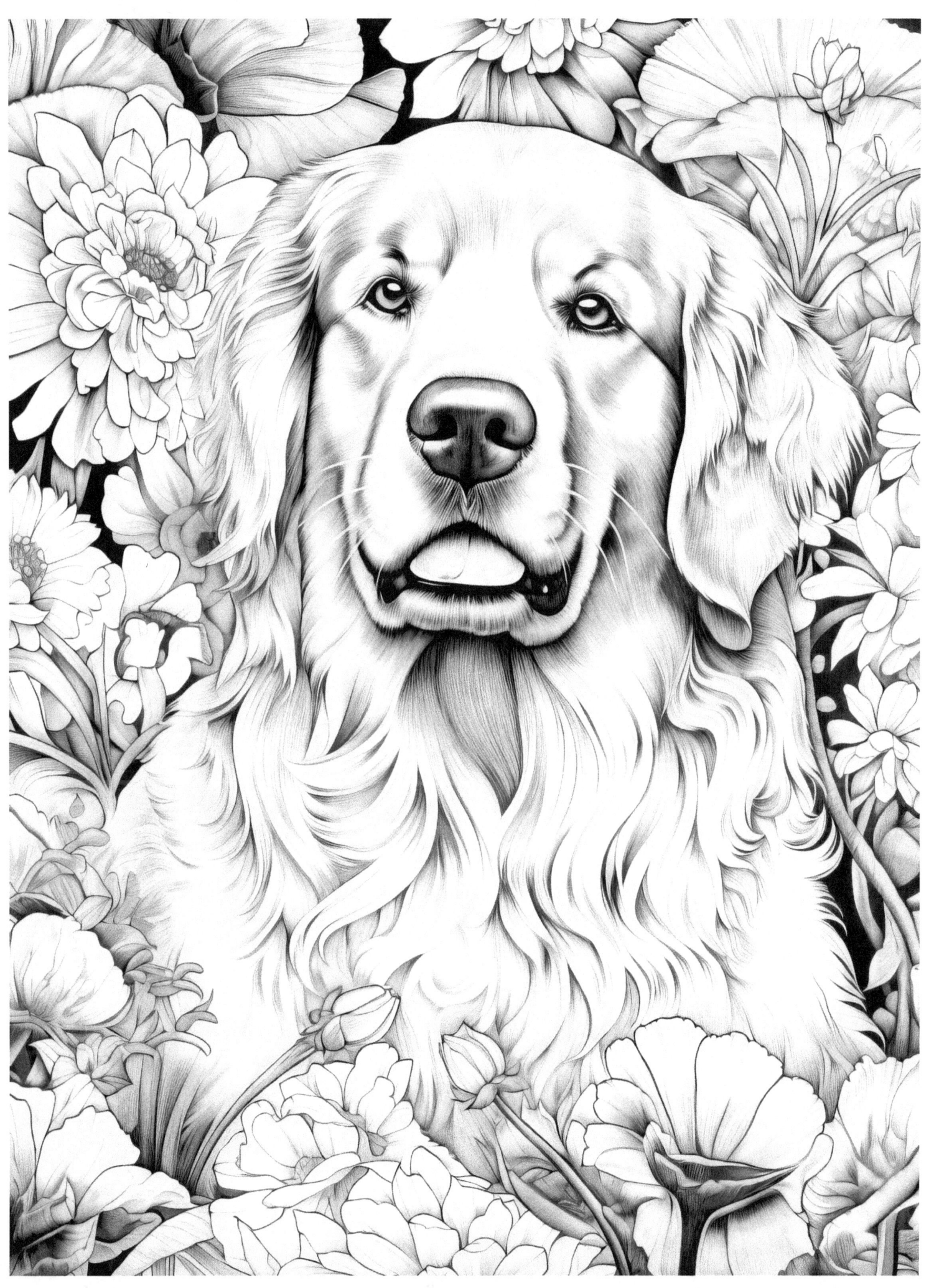

THIS PAGE
INTENTIONALLY
LEFT BLANK.

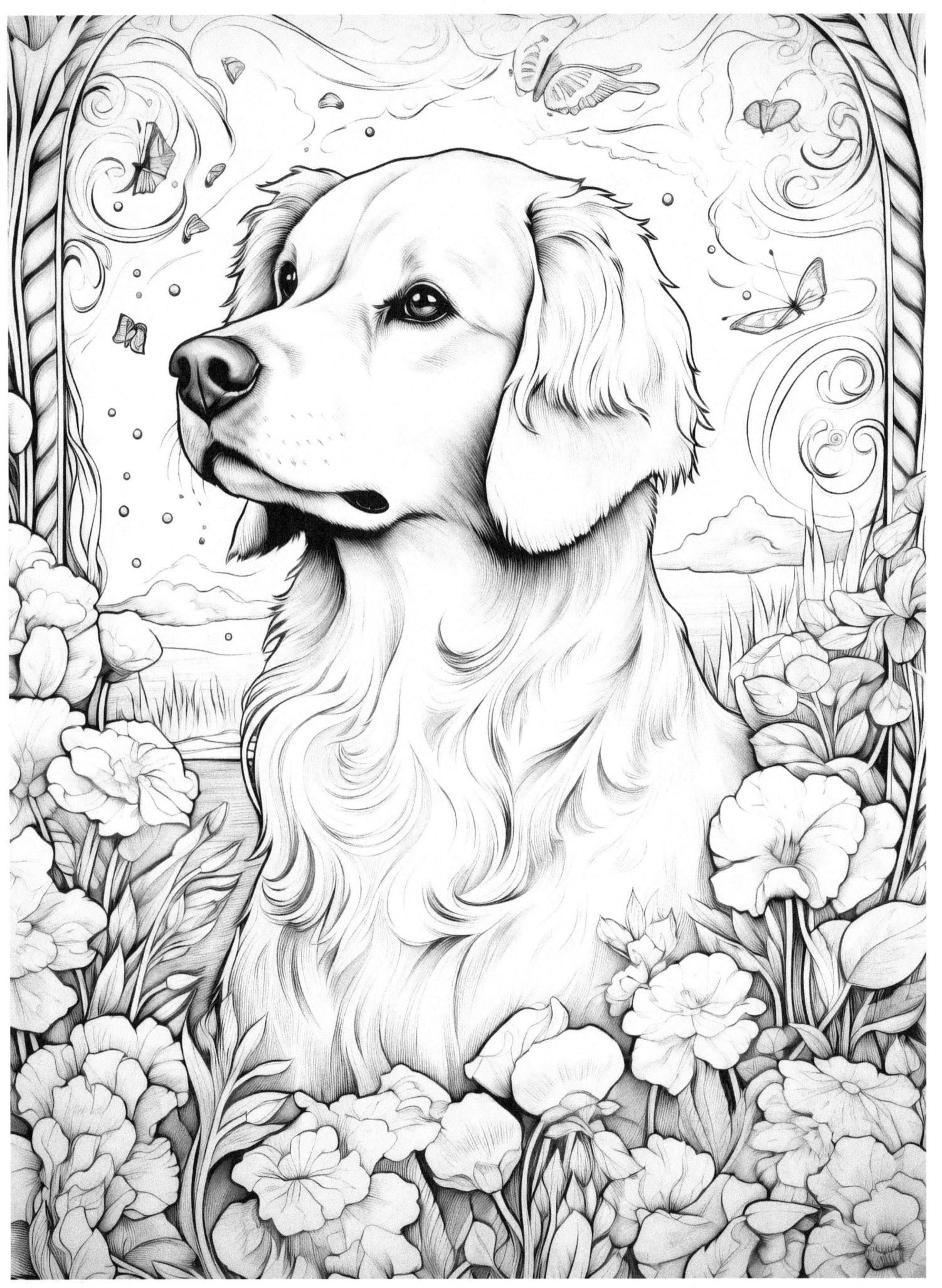

THIS PAGE
INTENTIONALLY
LEFT BLANK.

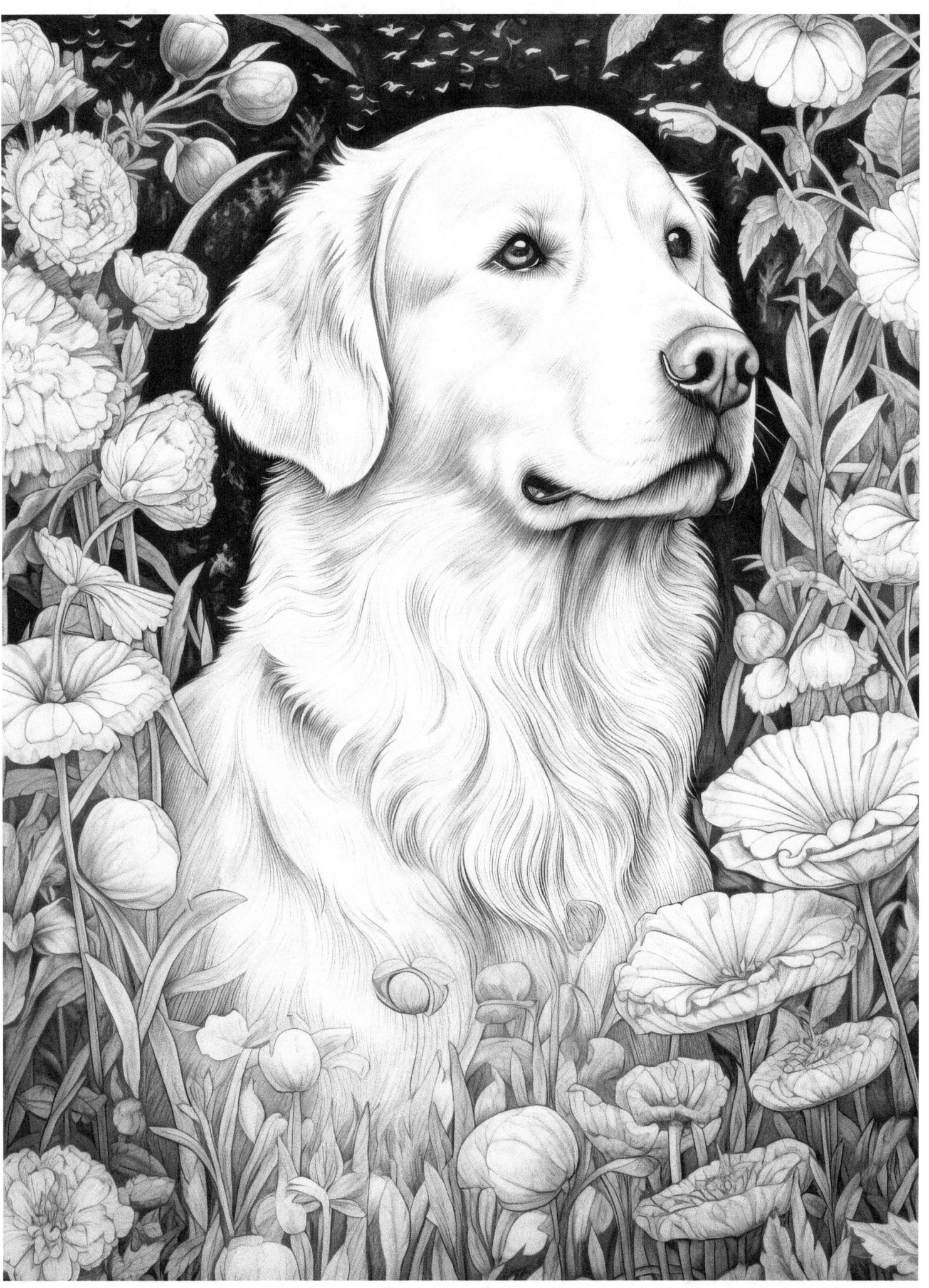

THIS PAGE
INTENTIONALLY
LEFT BLANK.

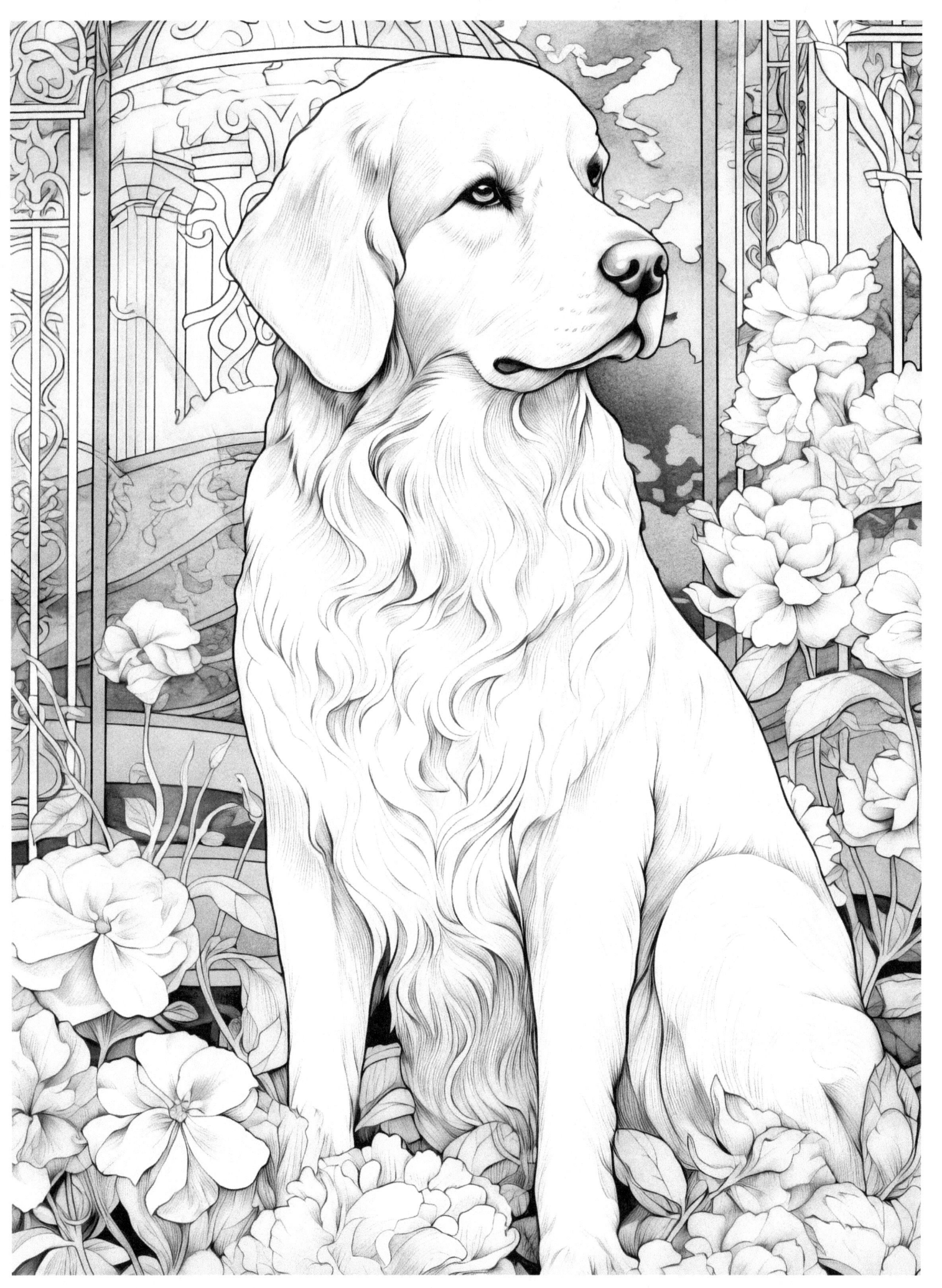

THIS PAGE INTENTIONALLY LEFT BLANK.

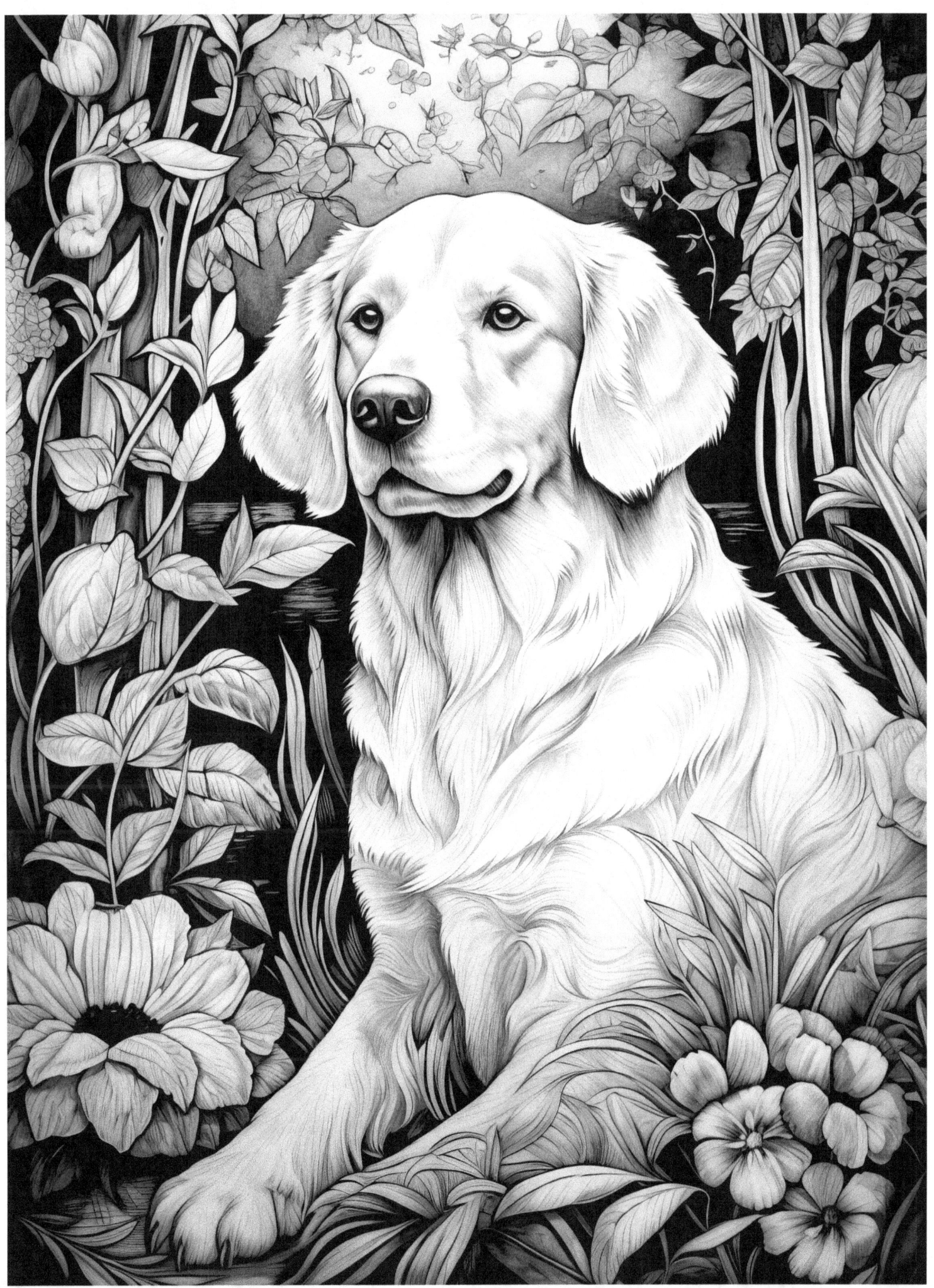

THIS PAGE
INTENTIONALLY
LEFT BLANK.

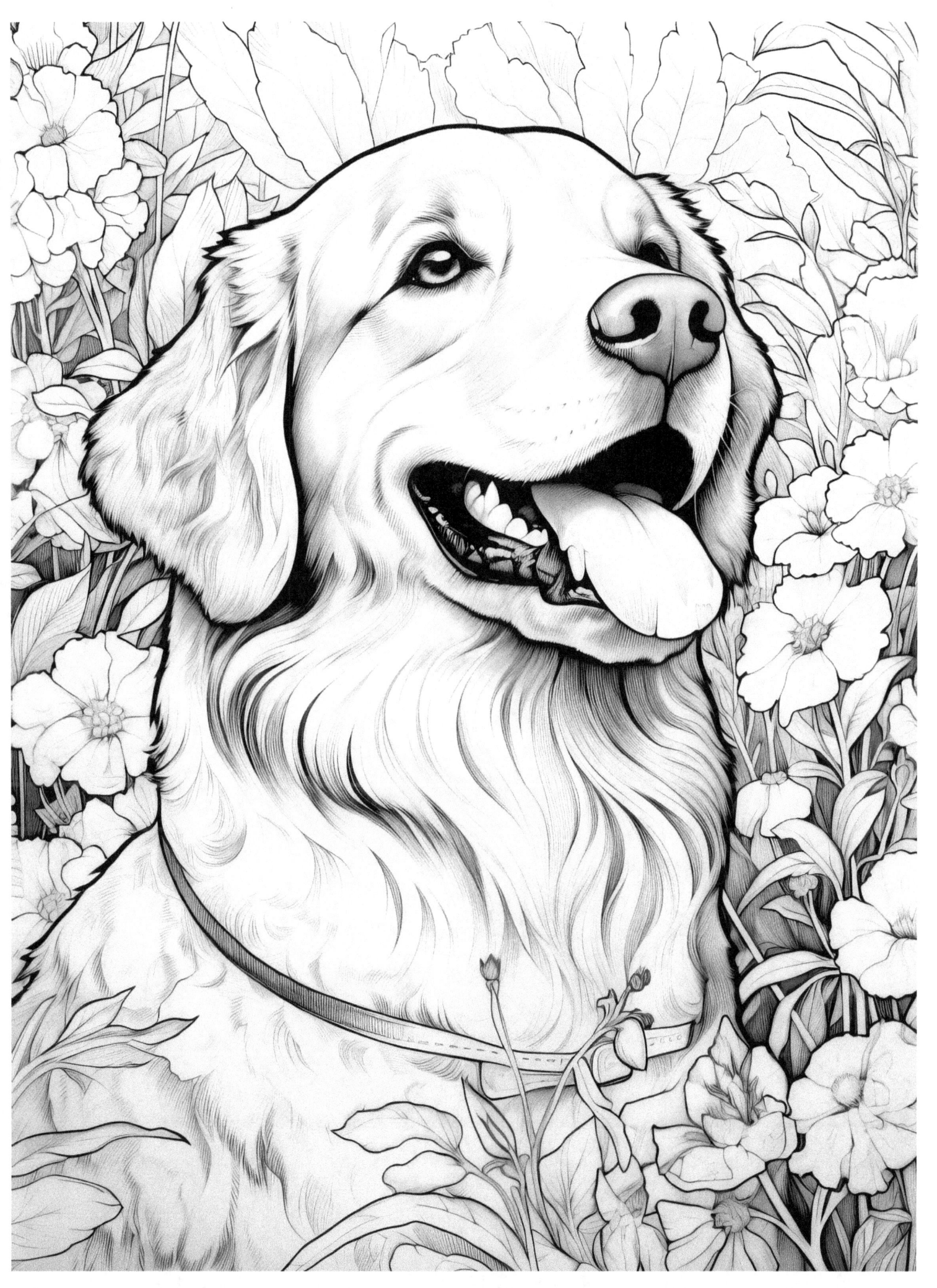

THIS PAGE
INTENTIONALLY
LEFT BLANK.

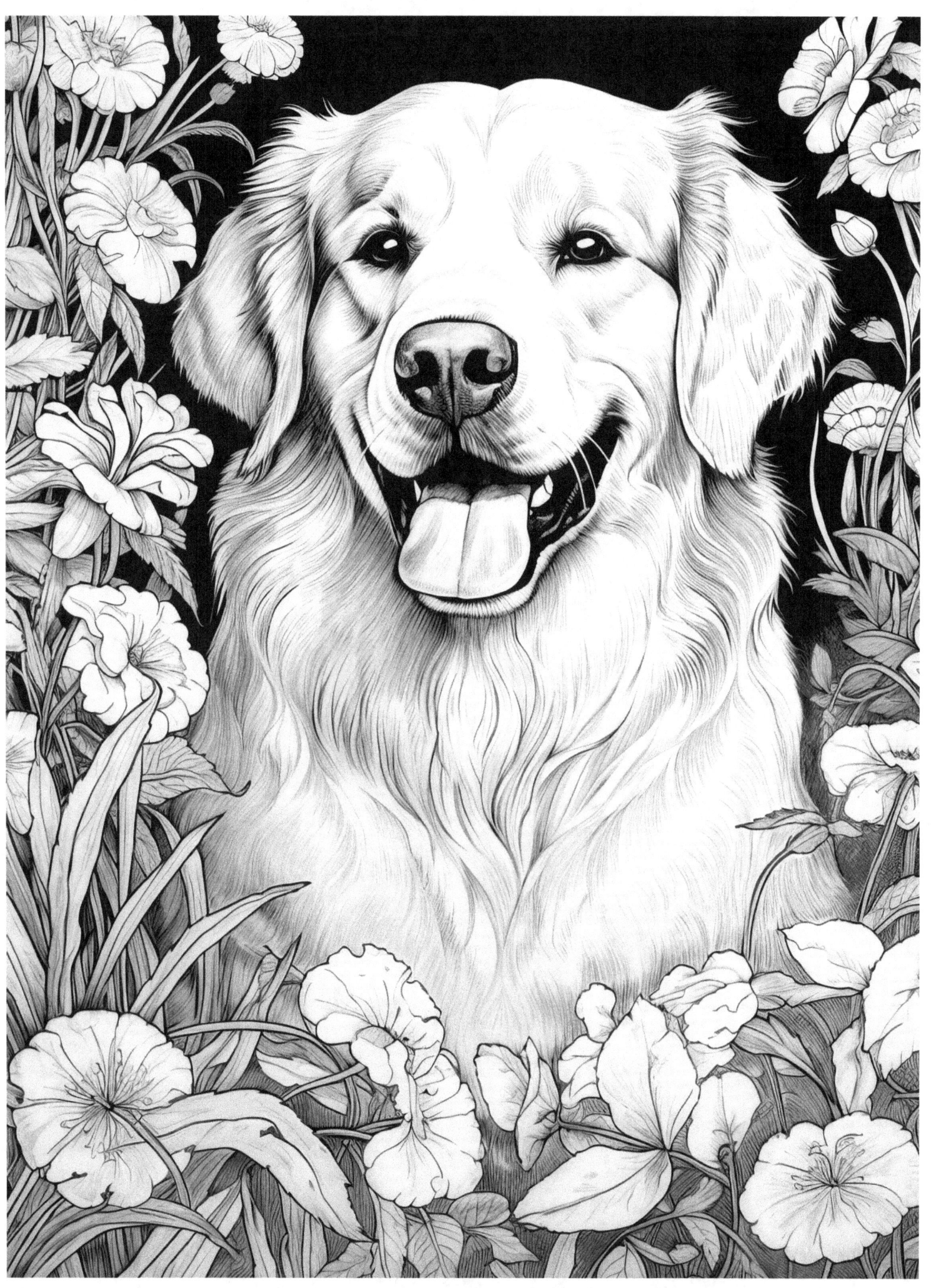

THIS PAGE
INTENTIONALLY
LEFT BLANK.

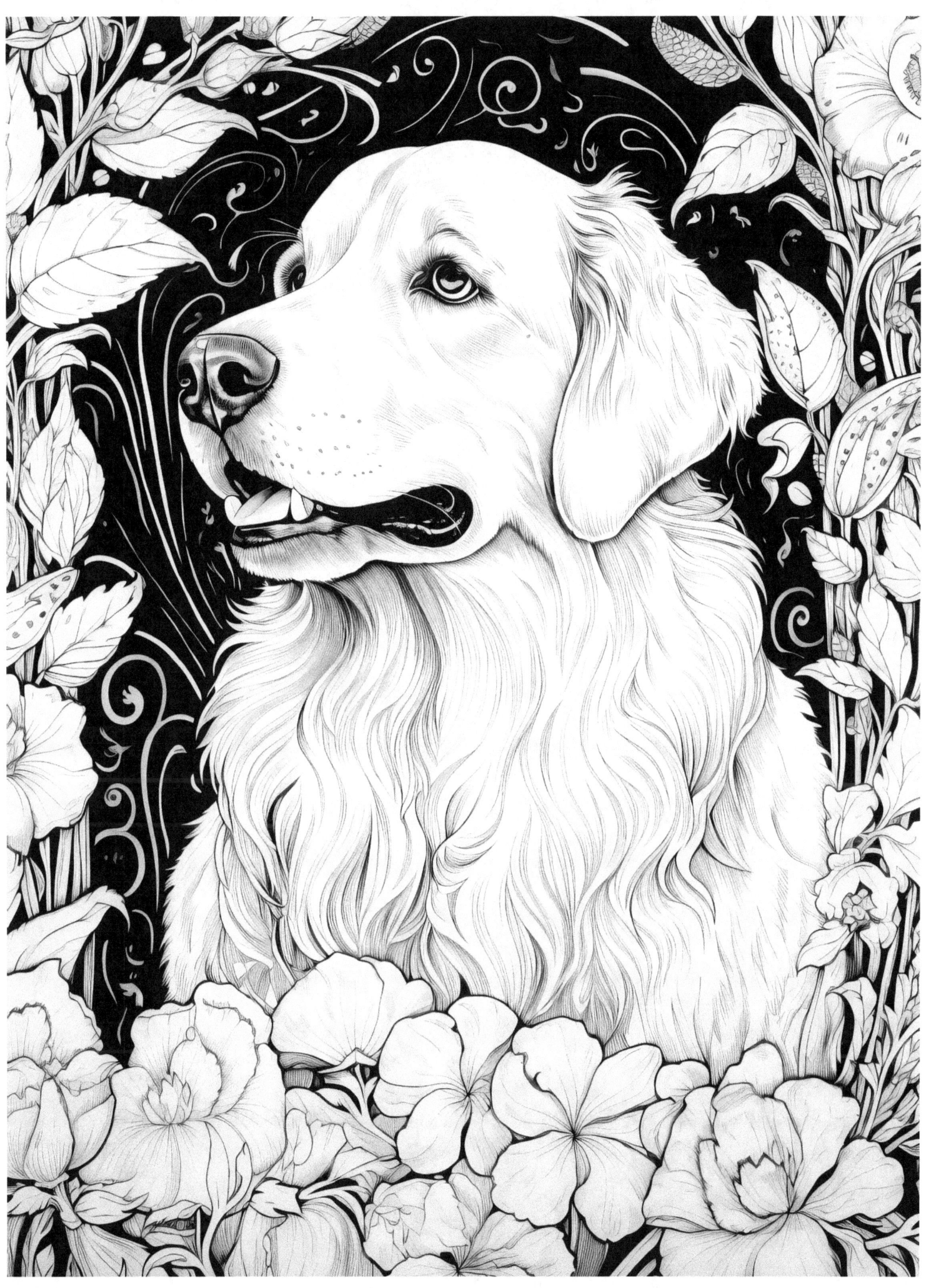

THIS PAGE
INTENTIONALLY
LEFT BLANK.

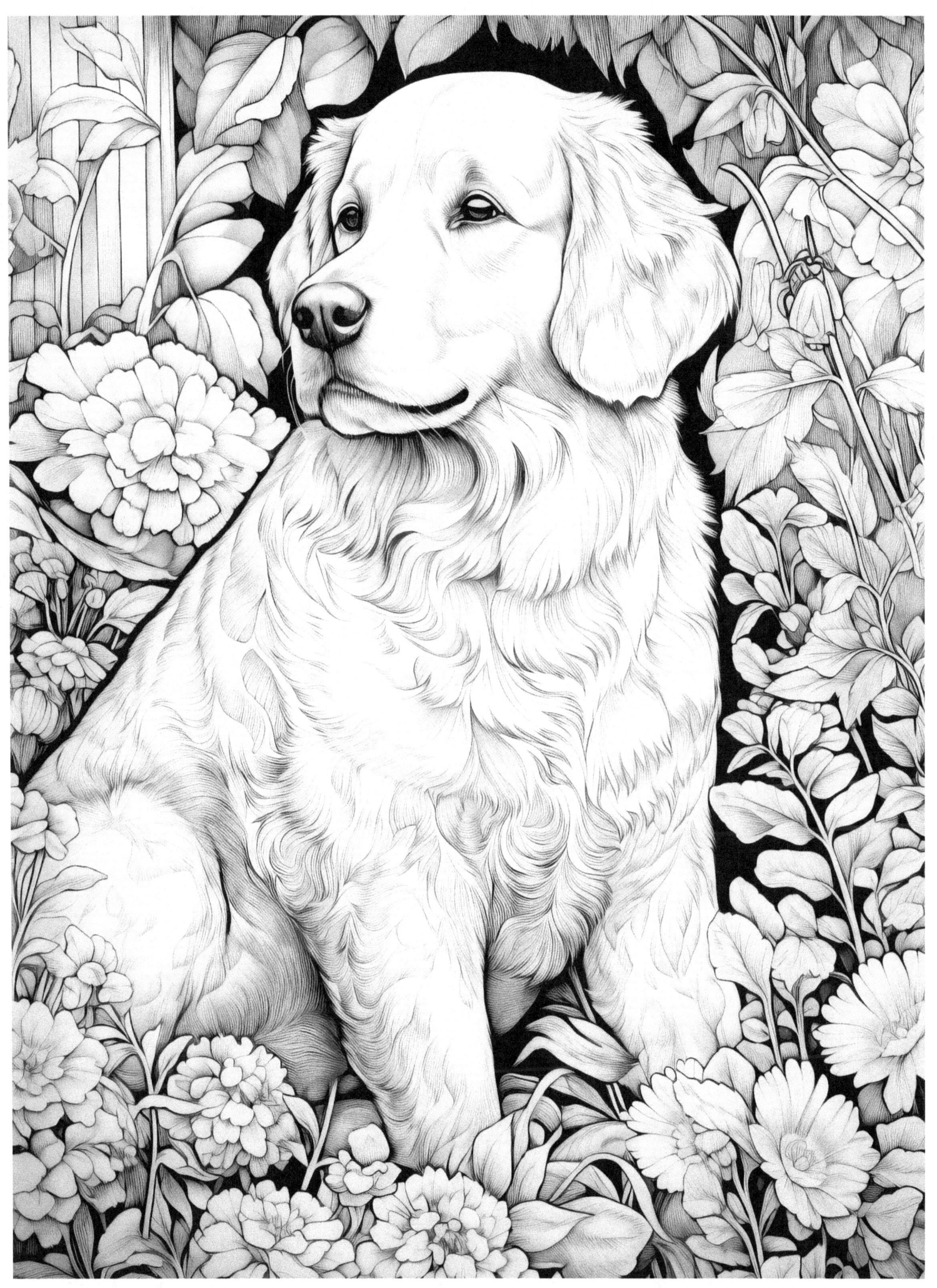

THIS PAGE
INTENTIONALLY
LEFT BLANK.

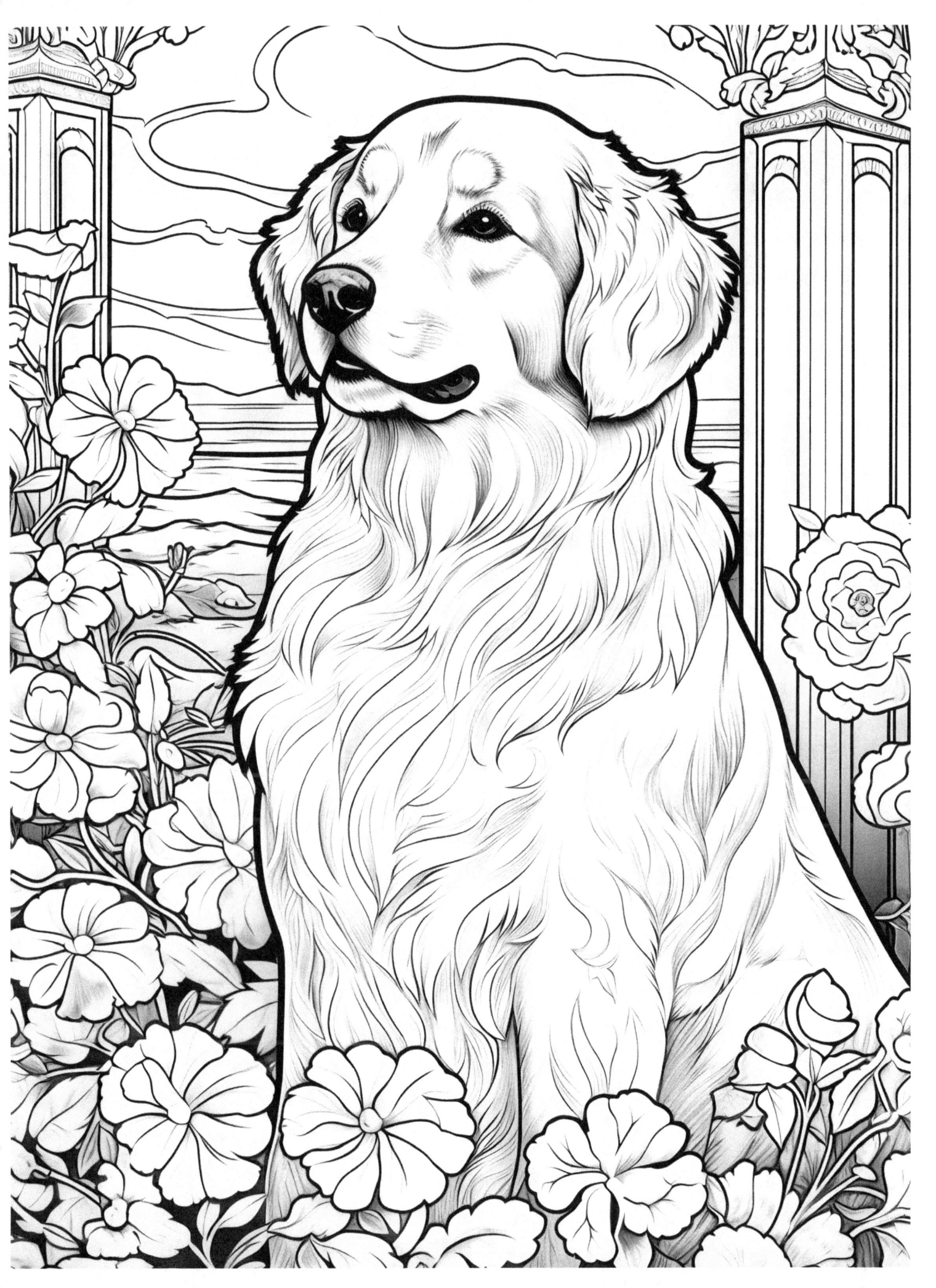

THIS PAGE
INTENTIONALLY
LEFT BLANK.

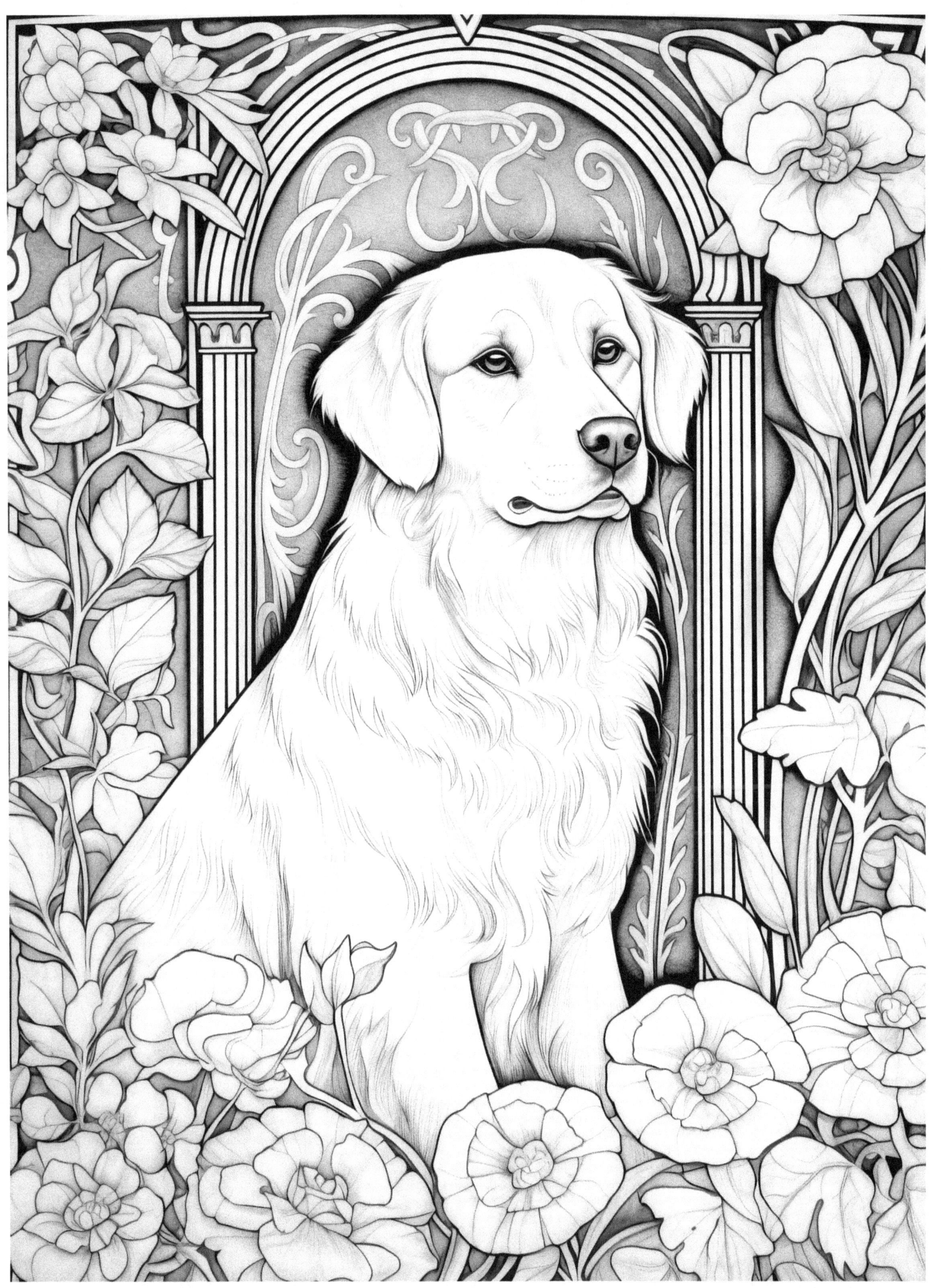

THIS PAGE
INTENTIONALLY
LEFT BLANK.

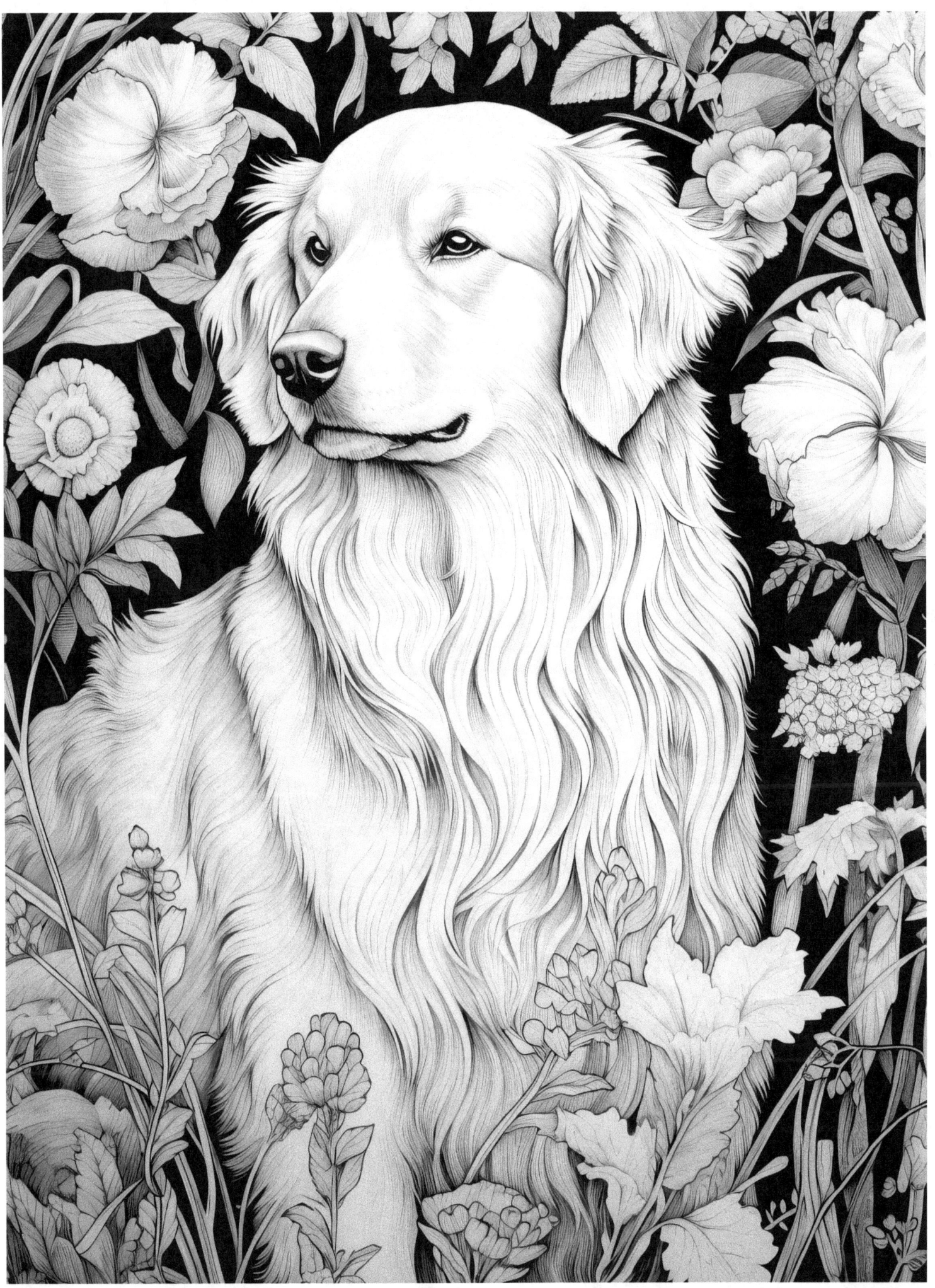

THIS PAGE
INTENTIONALLY
LEFT BLANK.

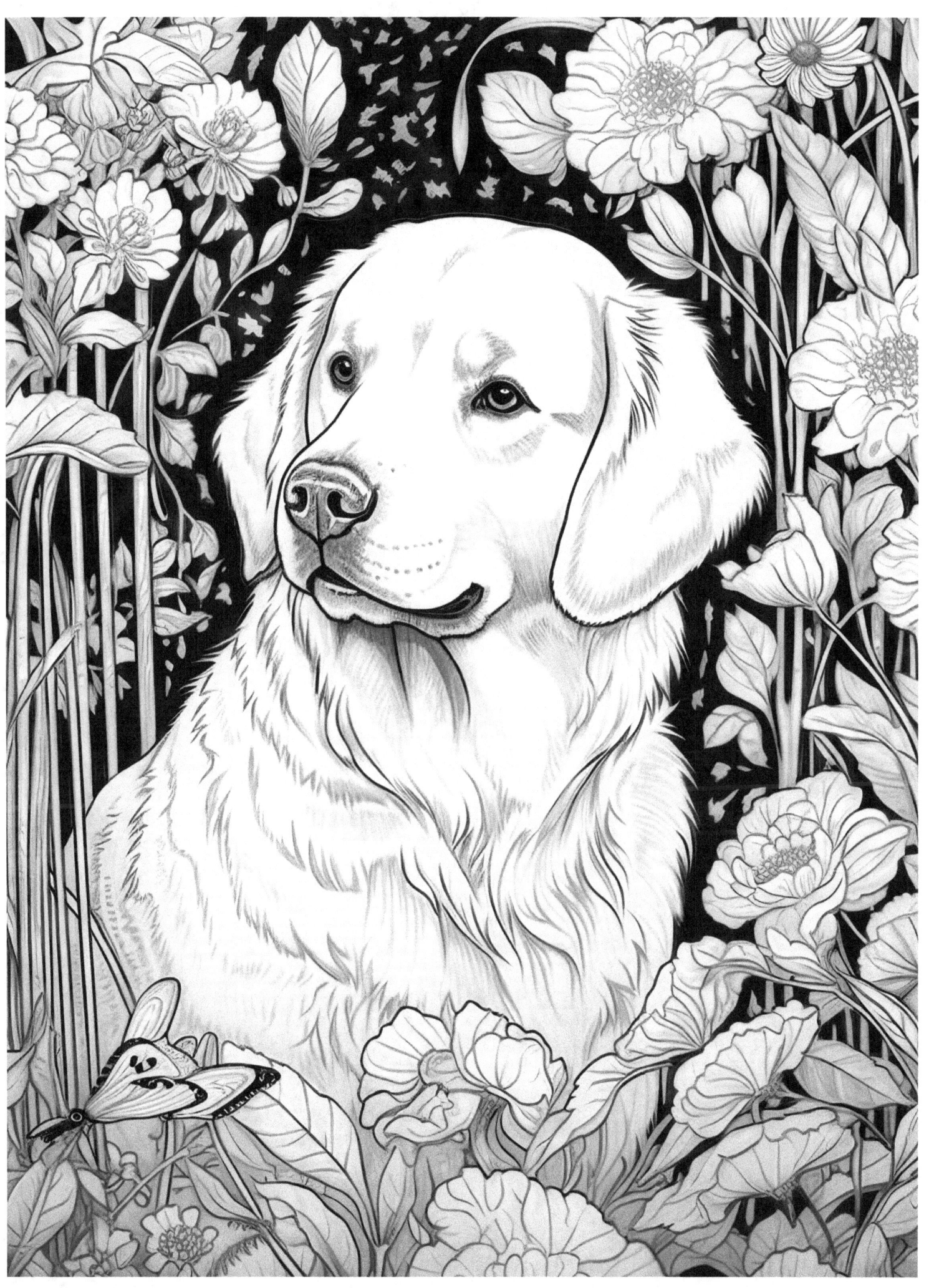

THIS PAGE
INTENTIONALLY
LEFT BLANK.

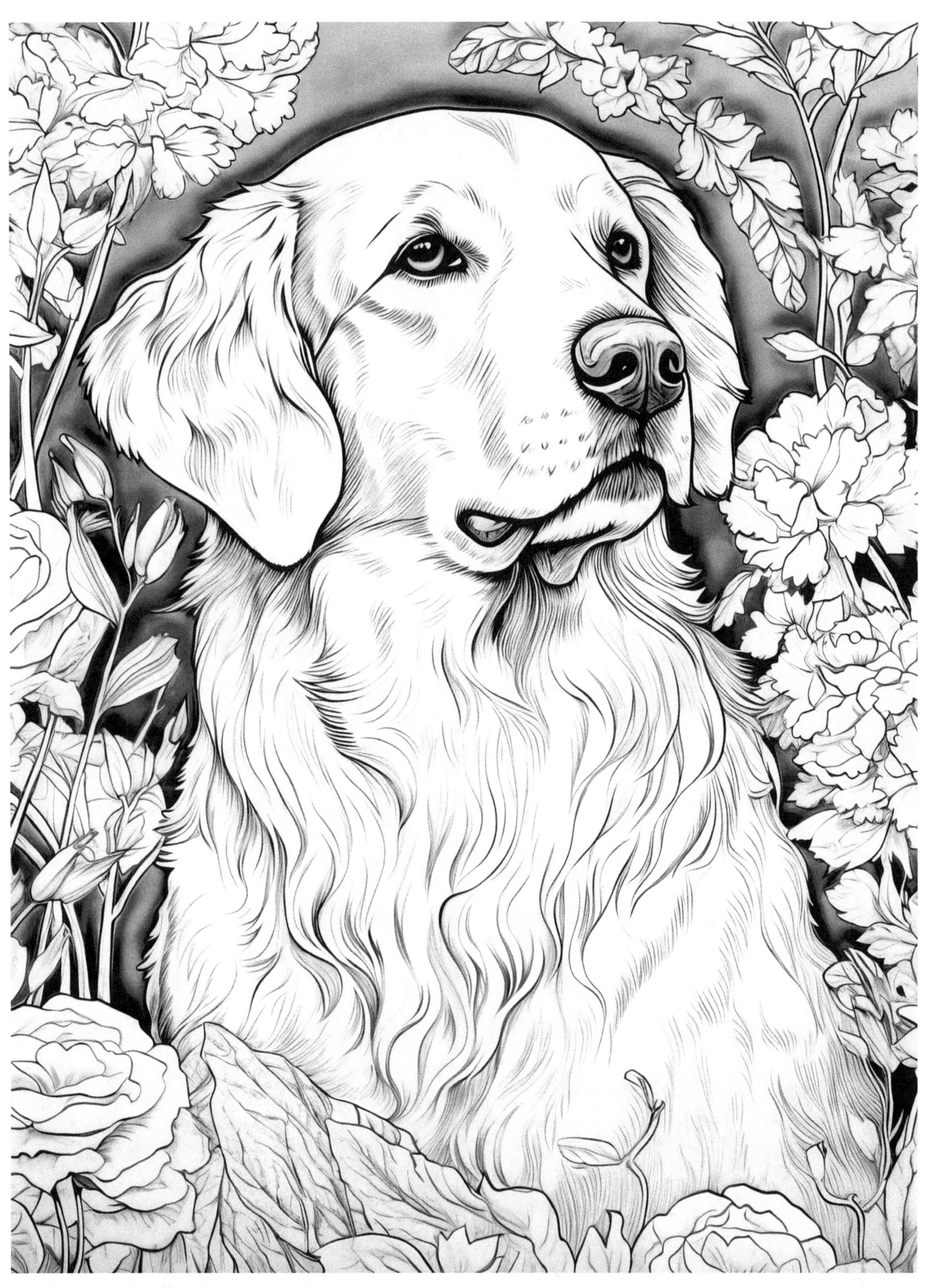

THIS PAGE
INTENTIONALLY
LEFT BLANK.

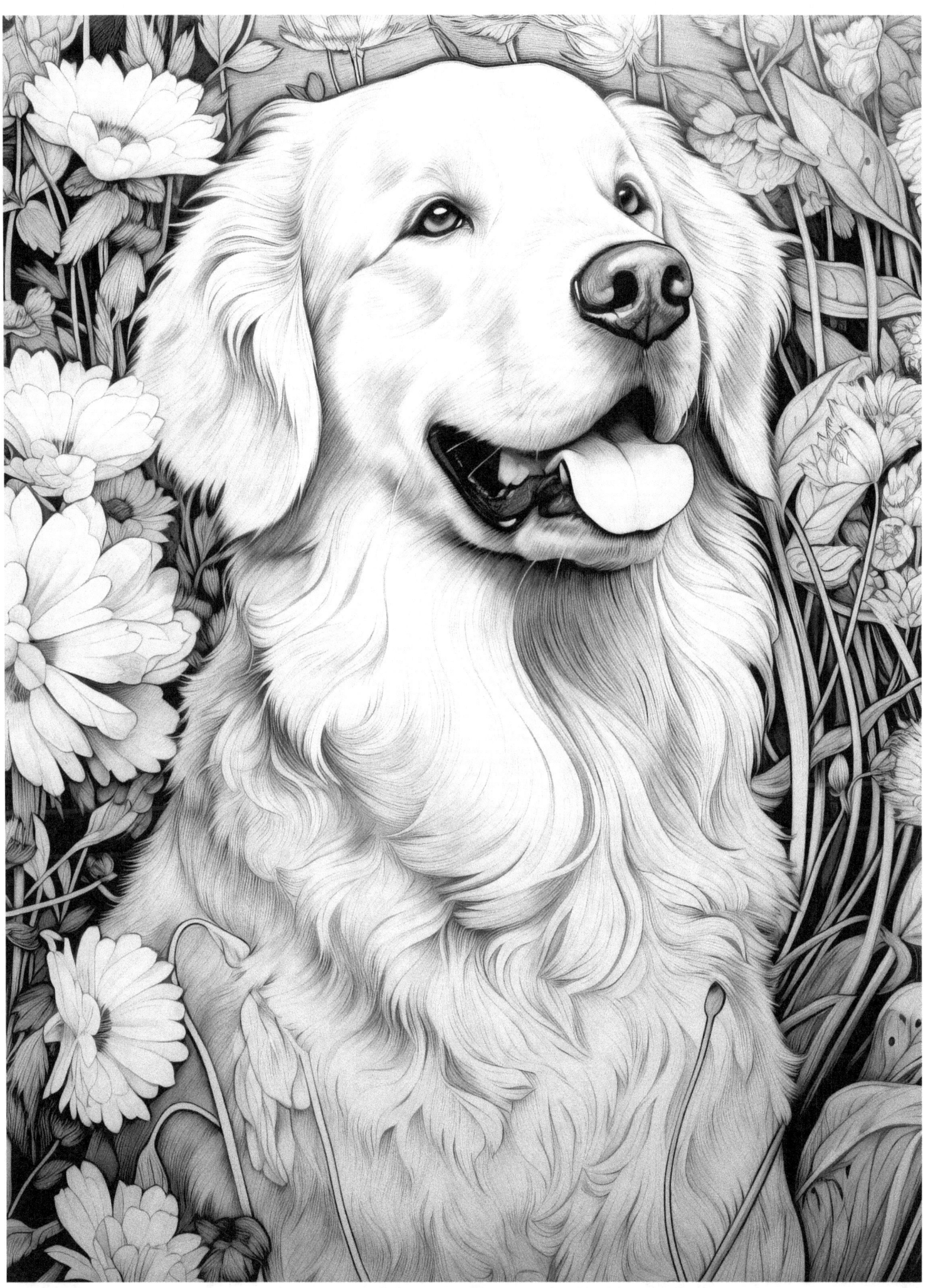

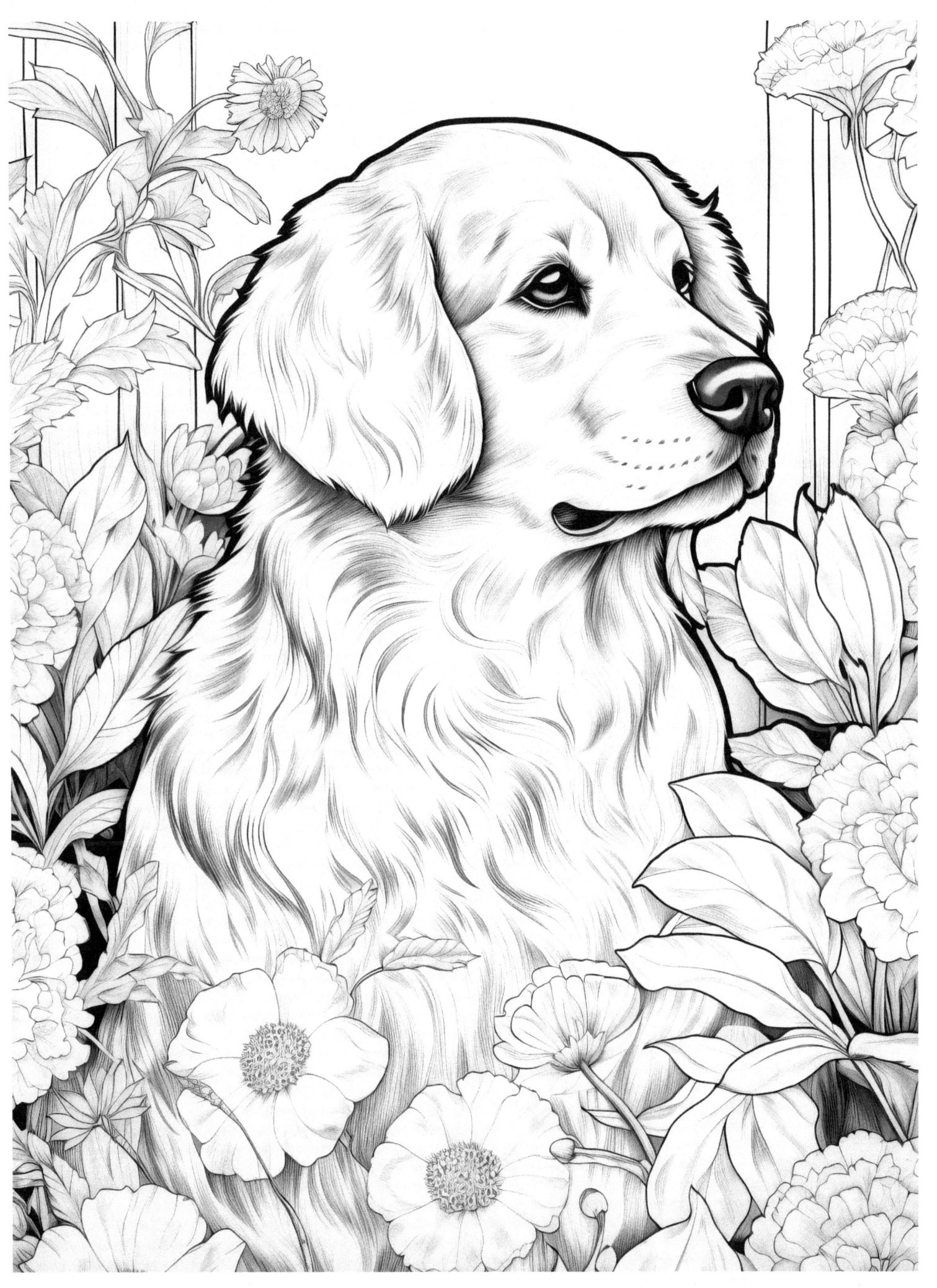

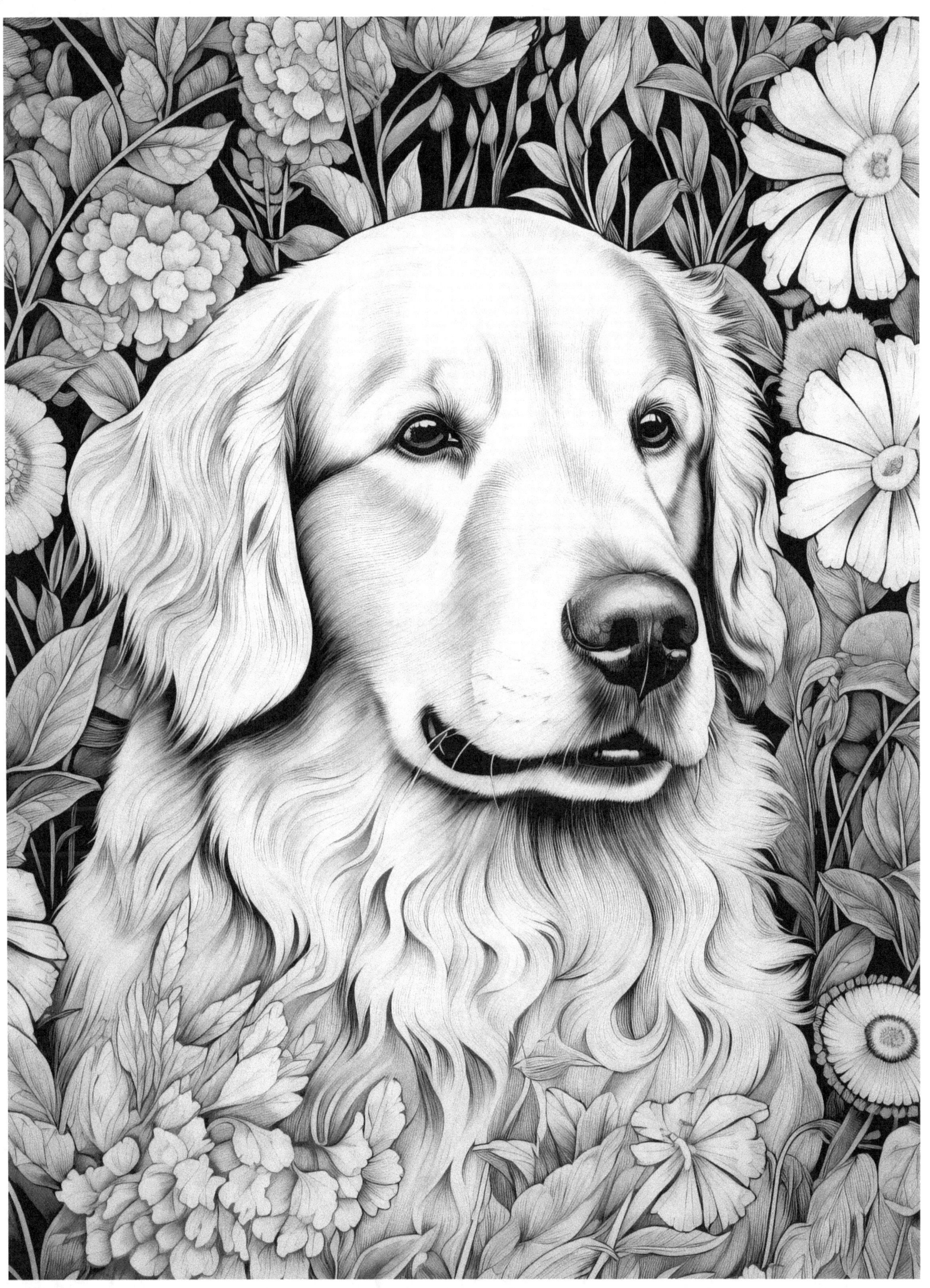

THIS PAGE INTENTIONALLY LEFT BLANK.

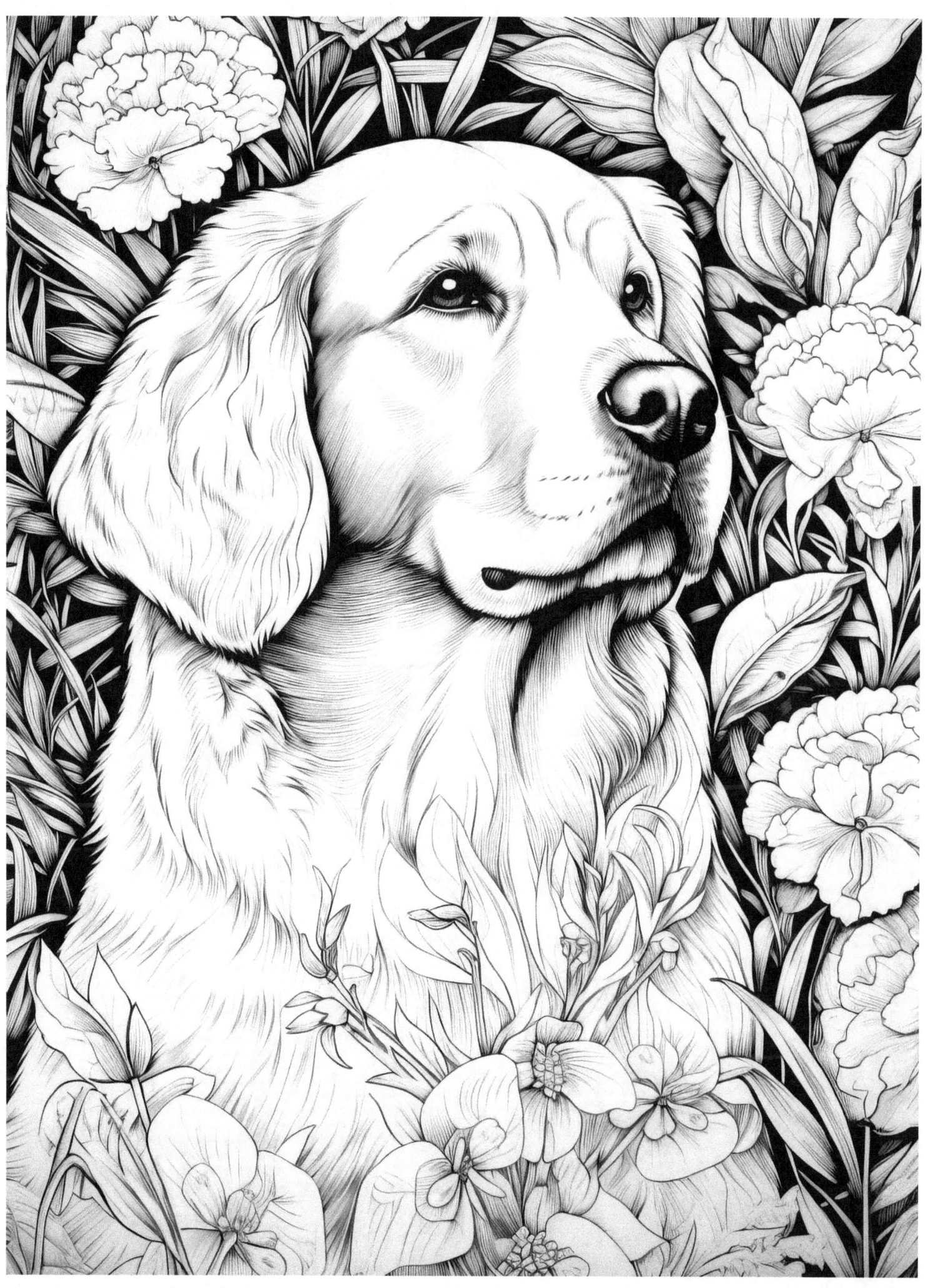

THIS PAGE
INTENTIONALLY
LEFT BLANK.

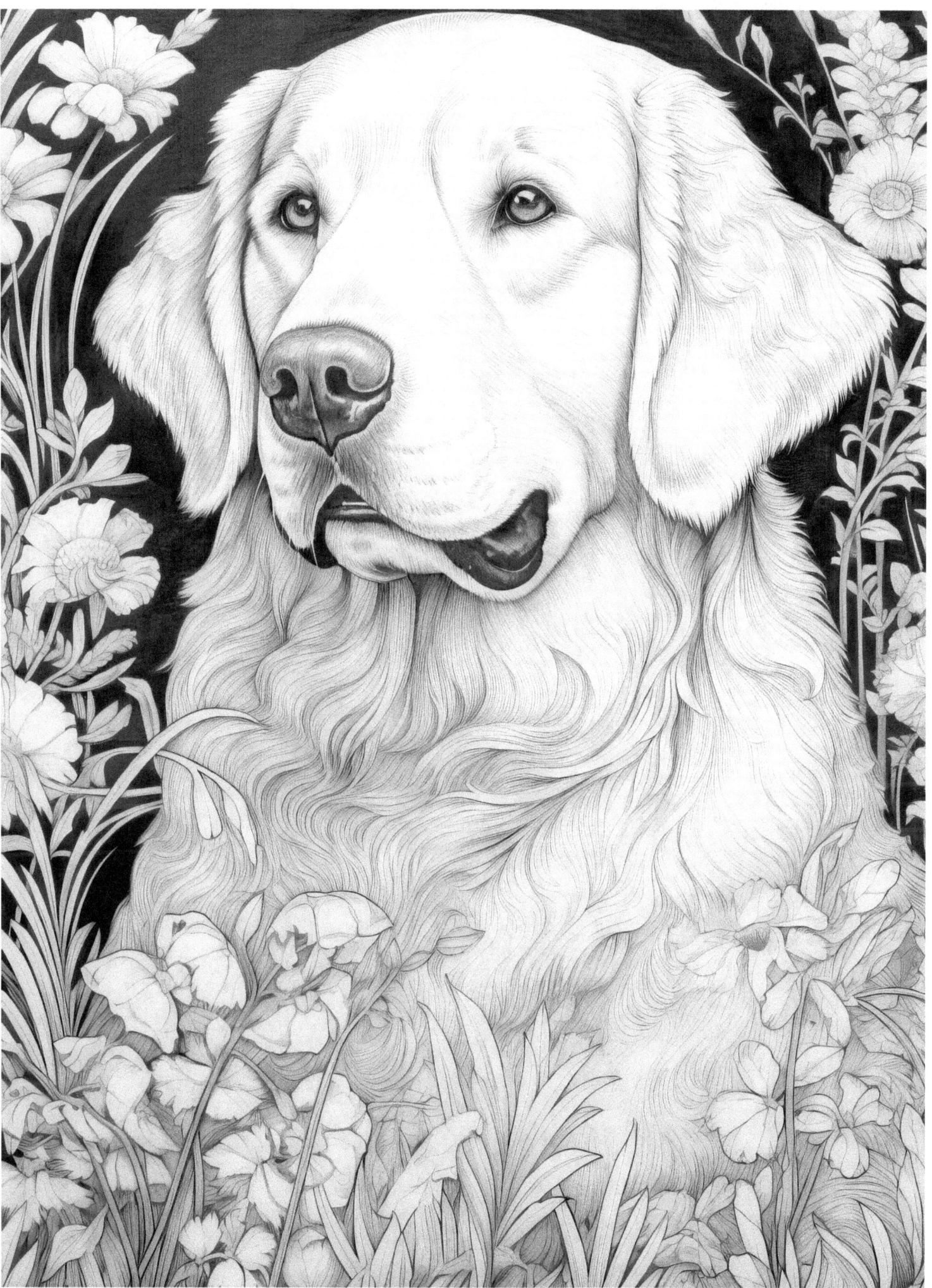

THIS PAGE
INTENTIONALLY
LEFT BLANK.

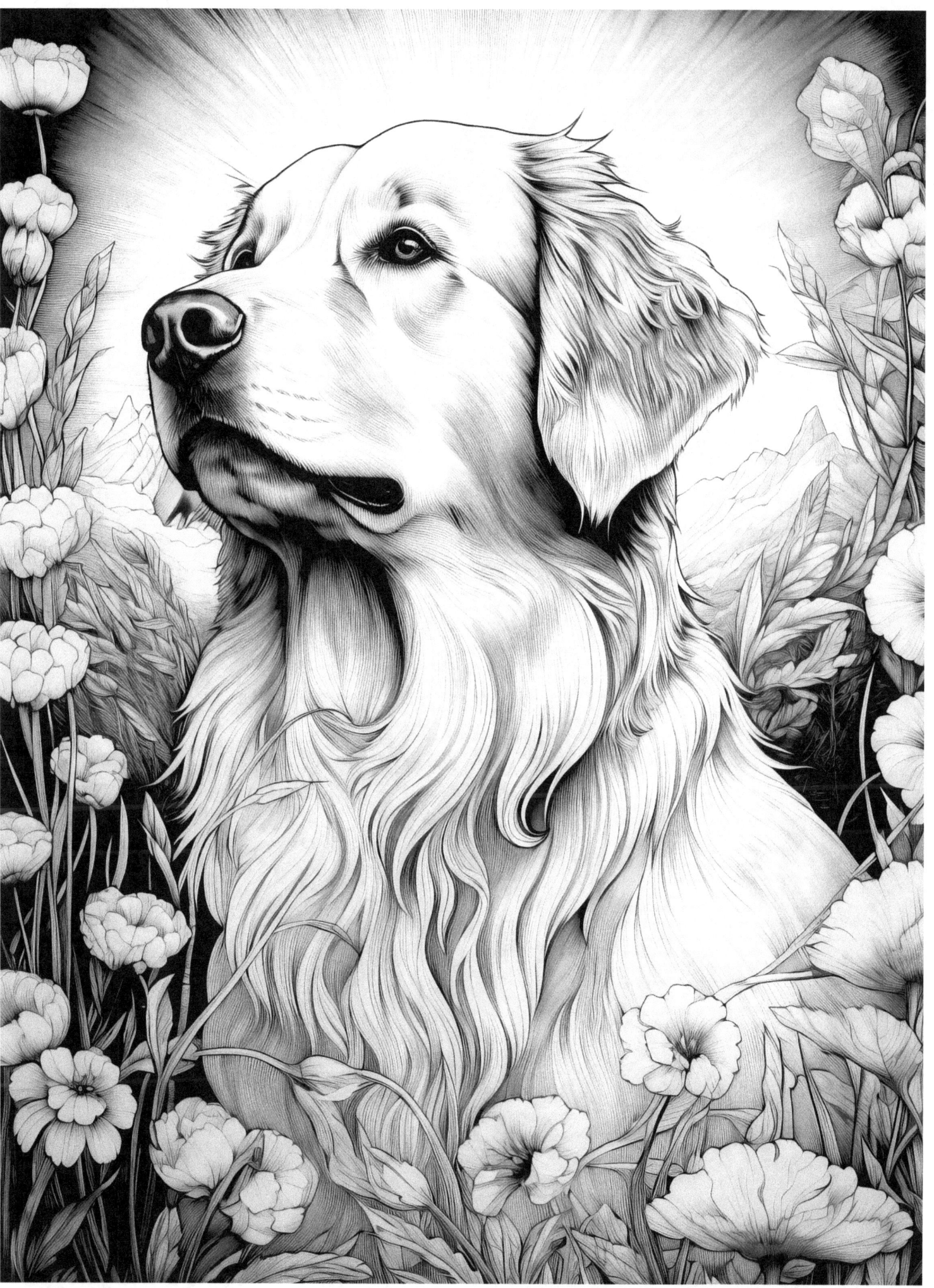

THIS PAGE
INTENTIONALLY
LEFT BLANK.

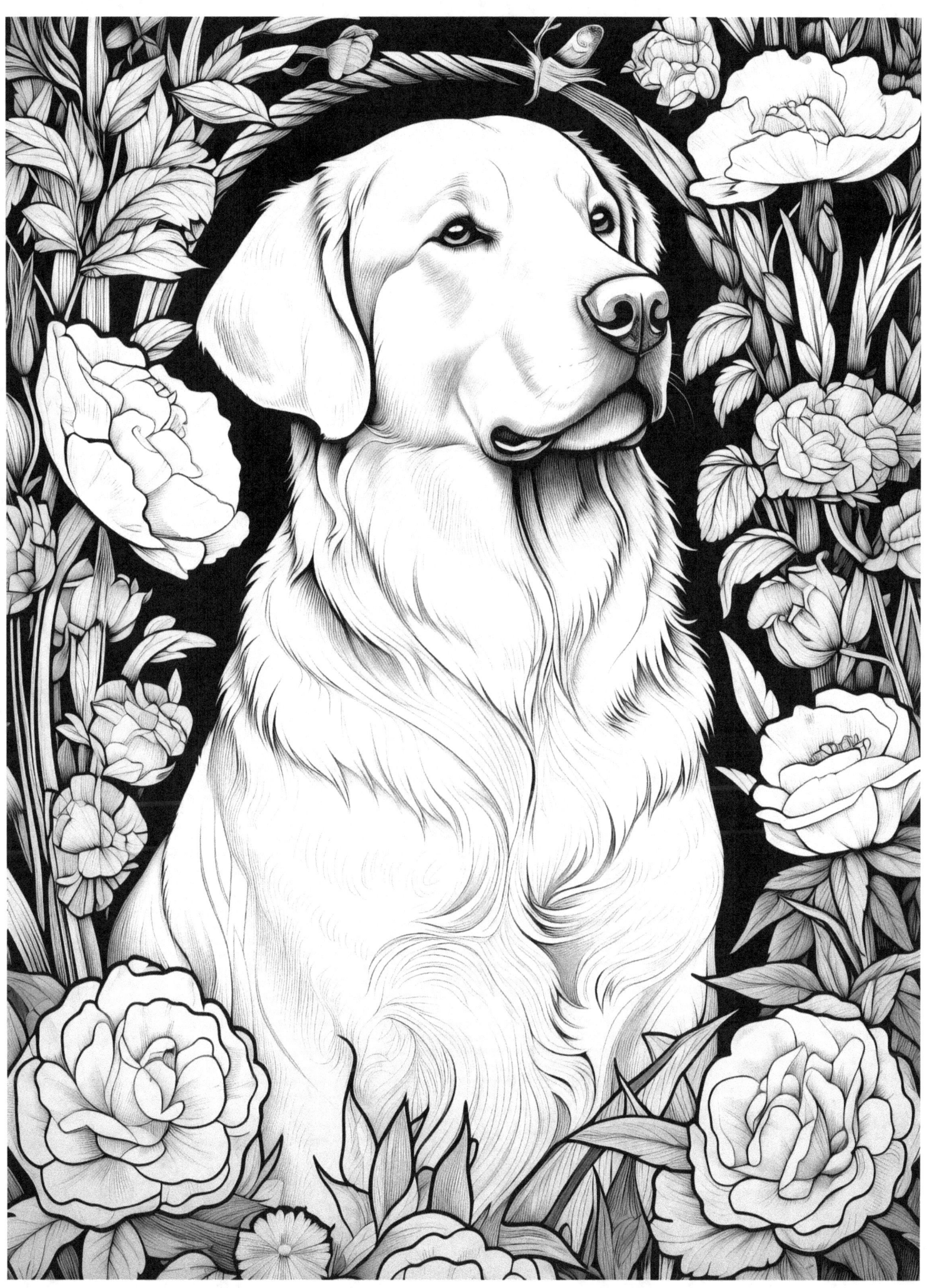

THIS PAGE
INTENTIONALLY
LEFT BLANK.

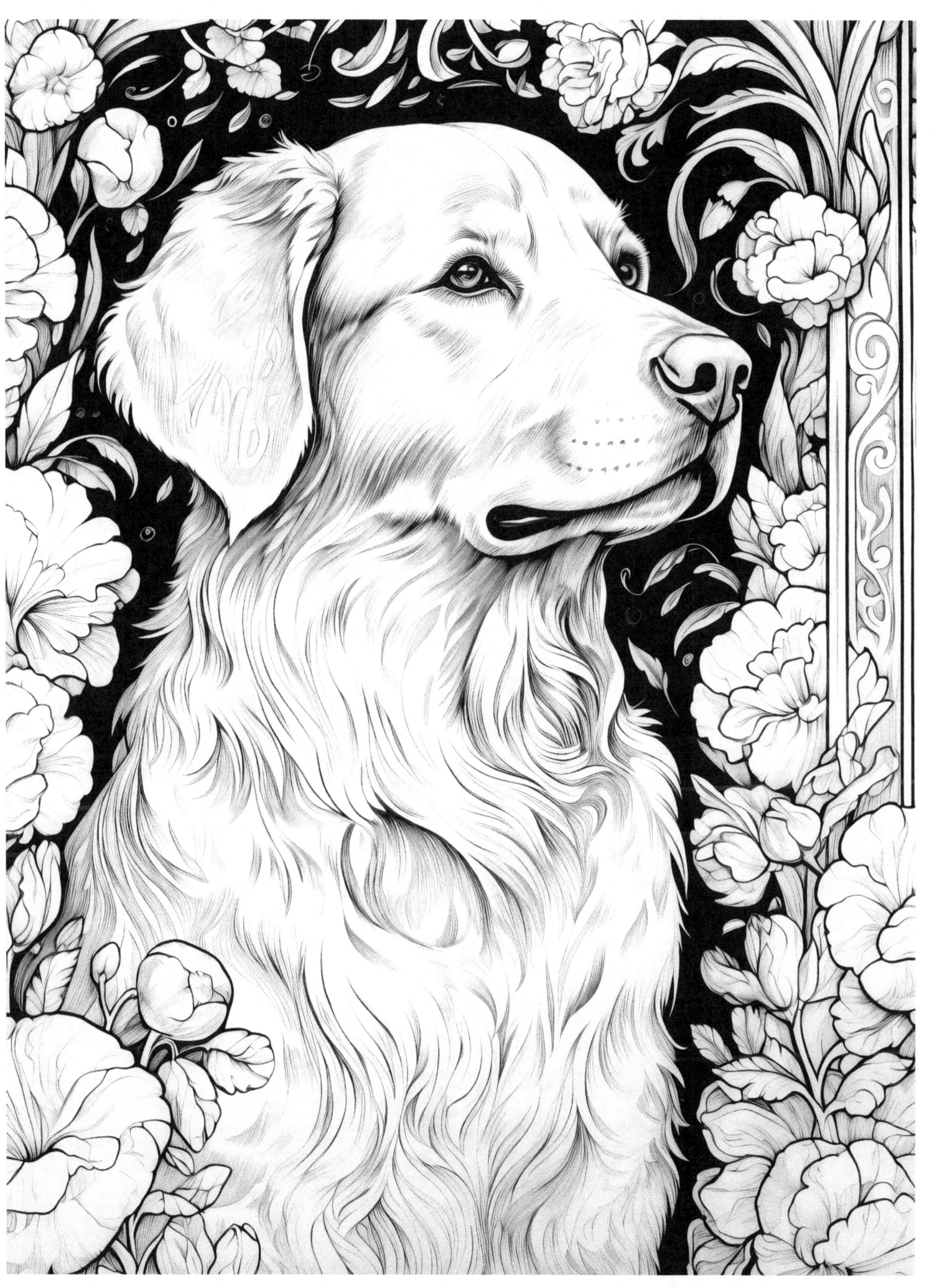

THIS PAGE INTENTIONALLY LEFT BLANK.

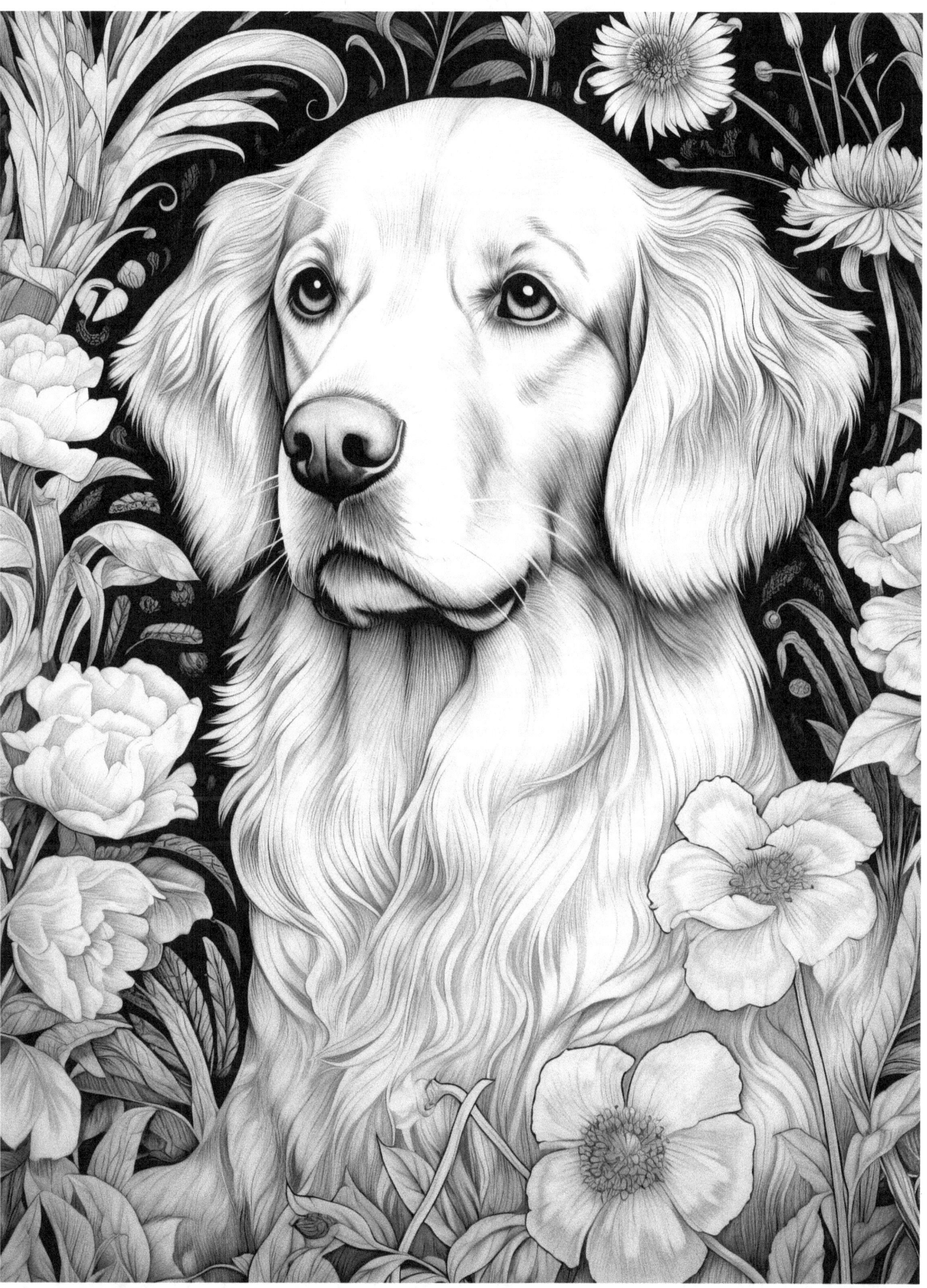

THIS PAGE
INTENTIONALLY
LEFT BLANK.

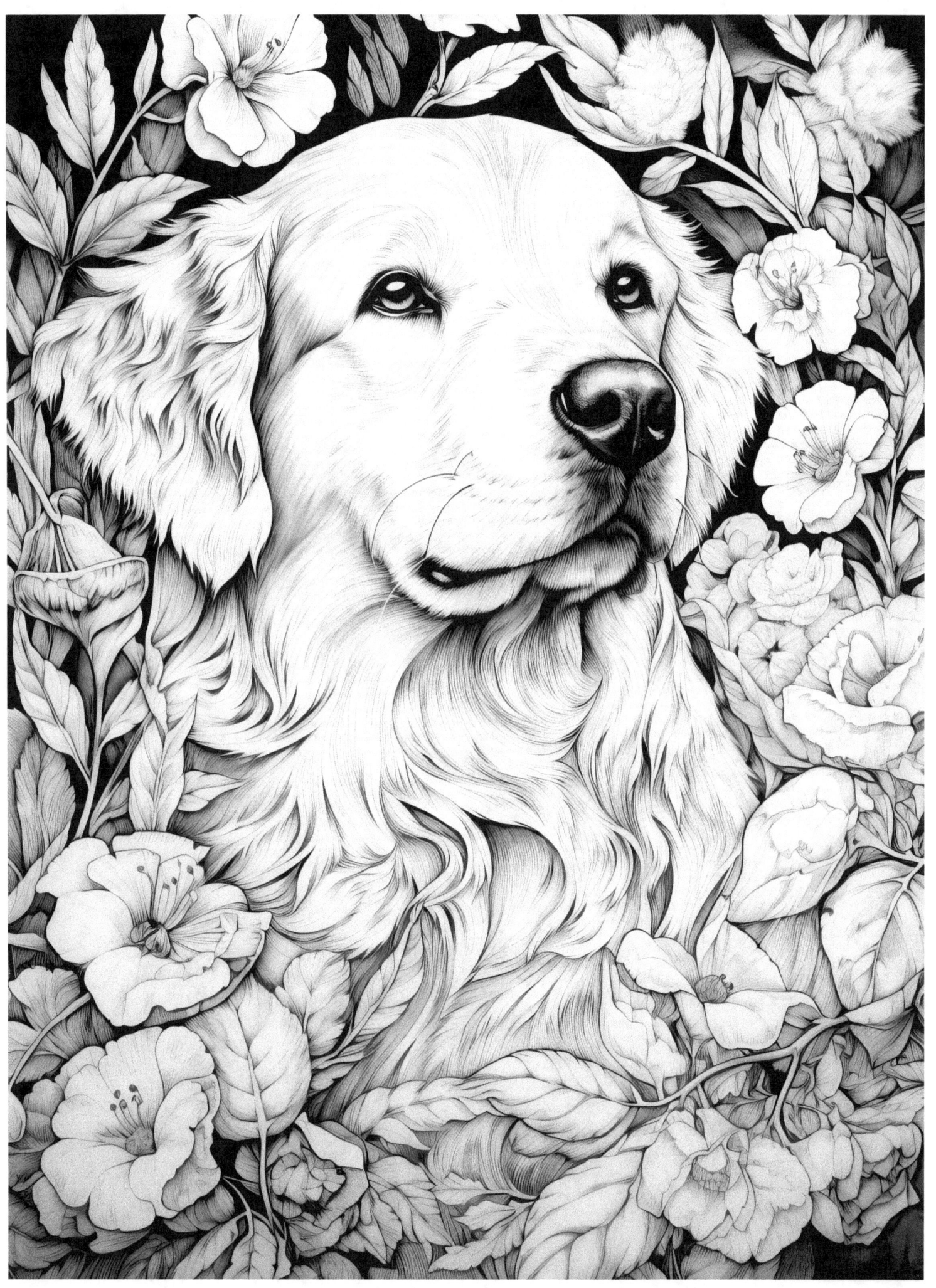

THIS PAGE
INTENTIONALLY
LEFT BLANK.

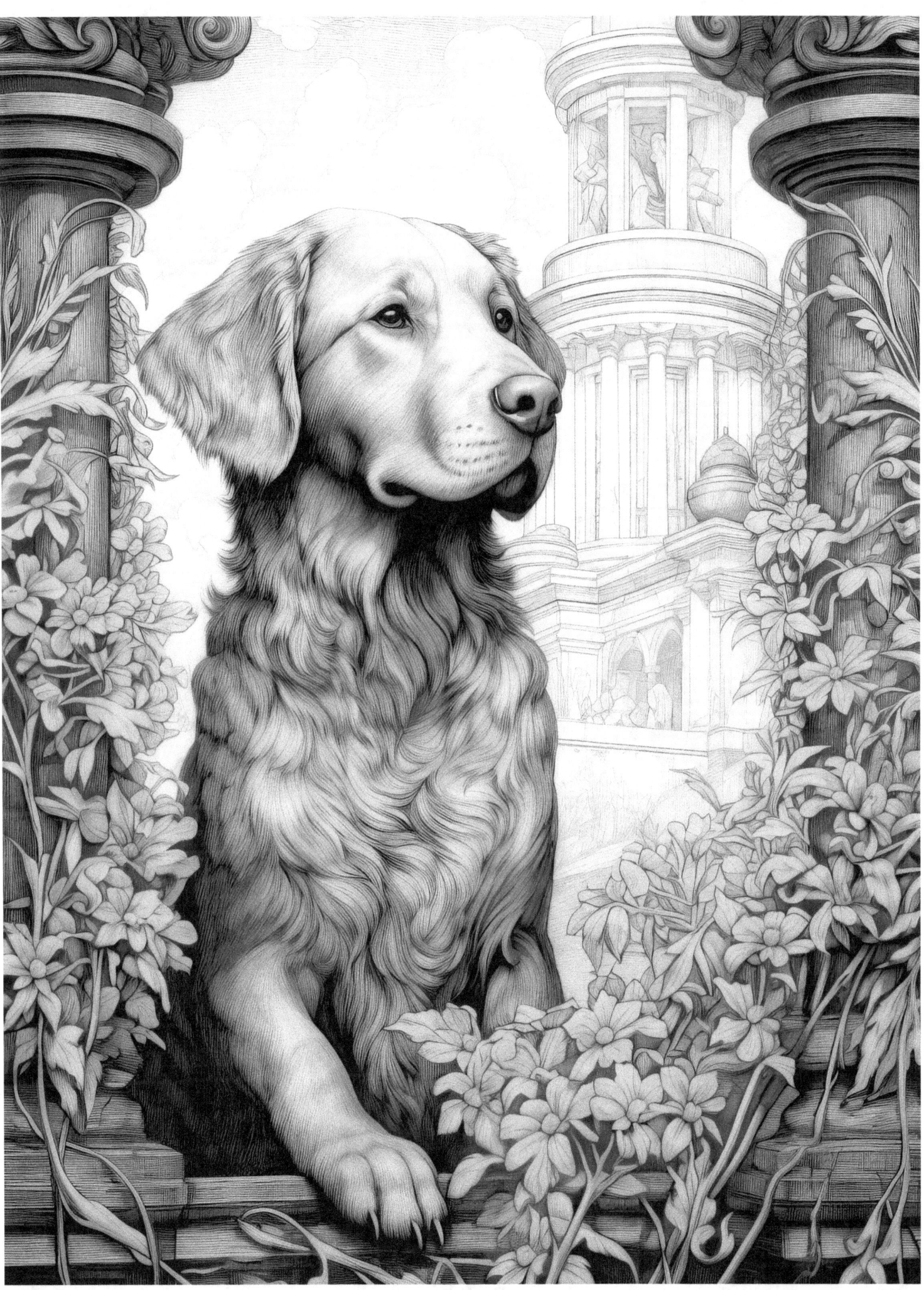

THIS PAGE
INTENTIONALLY
LEFT BLANK.

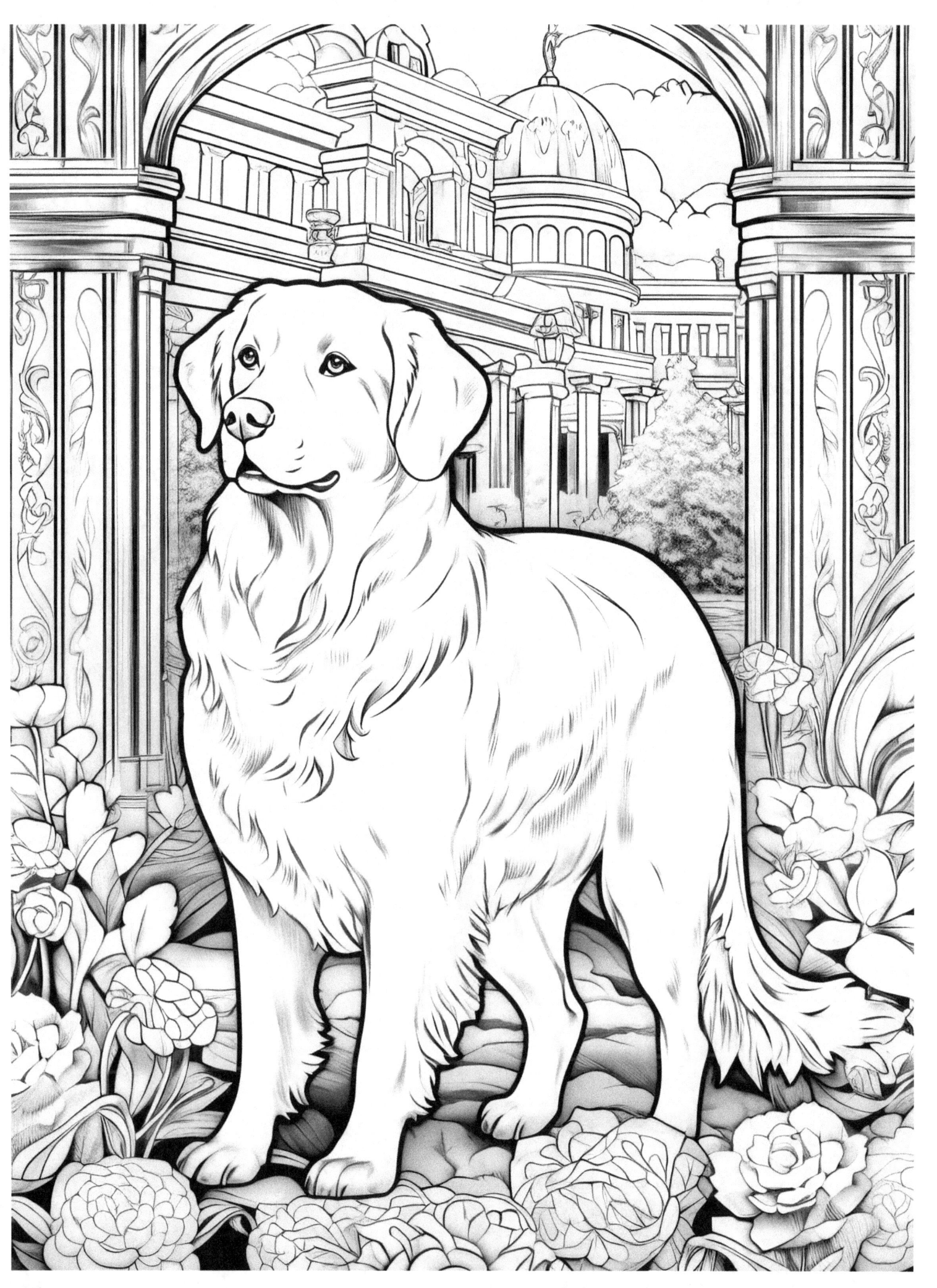

THIS PAGE
INTENTIONALLY
LEFT BLANK.

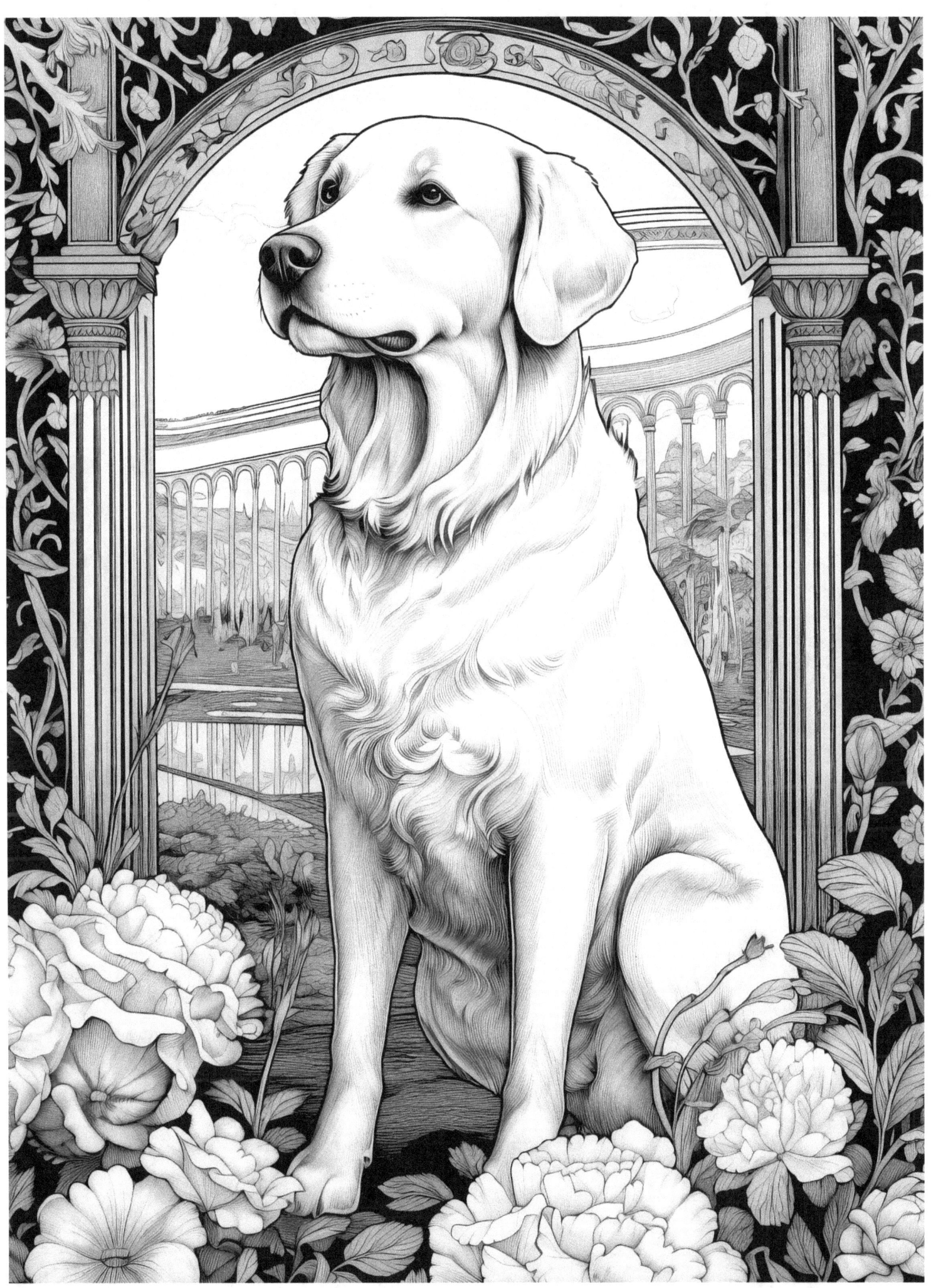

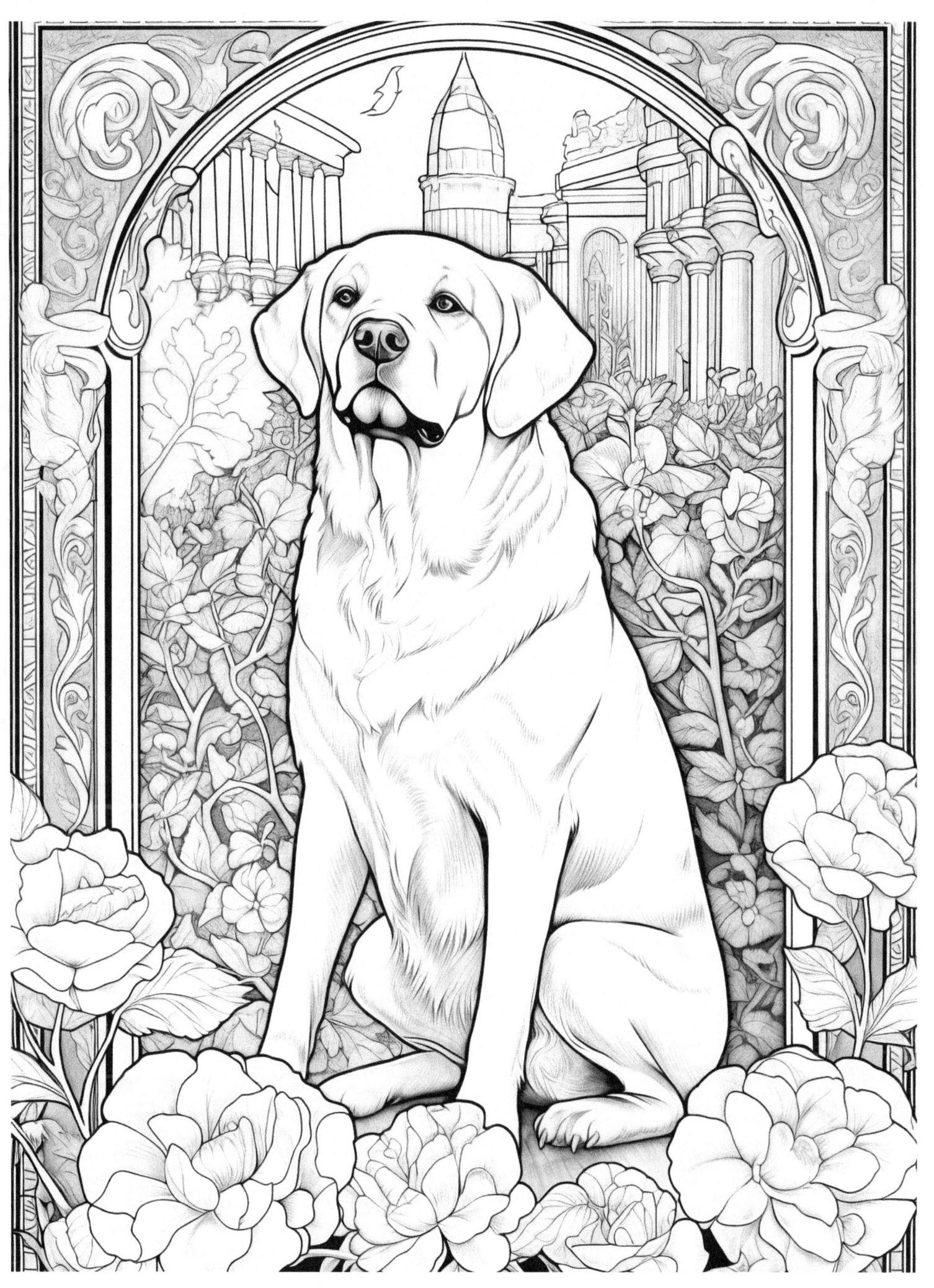

THIS PAGE INTENTIONALLY LEFT BLANK.

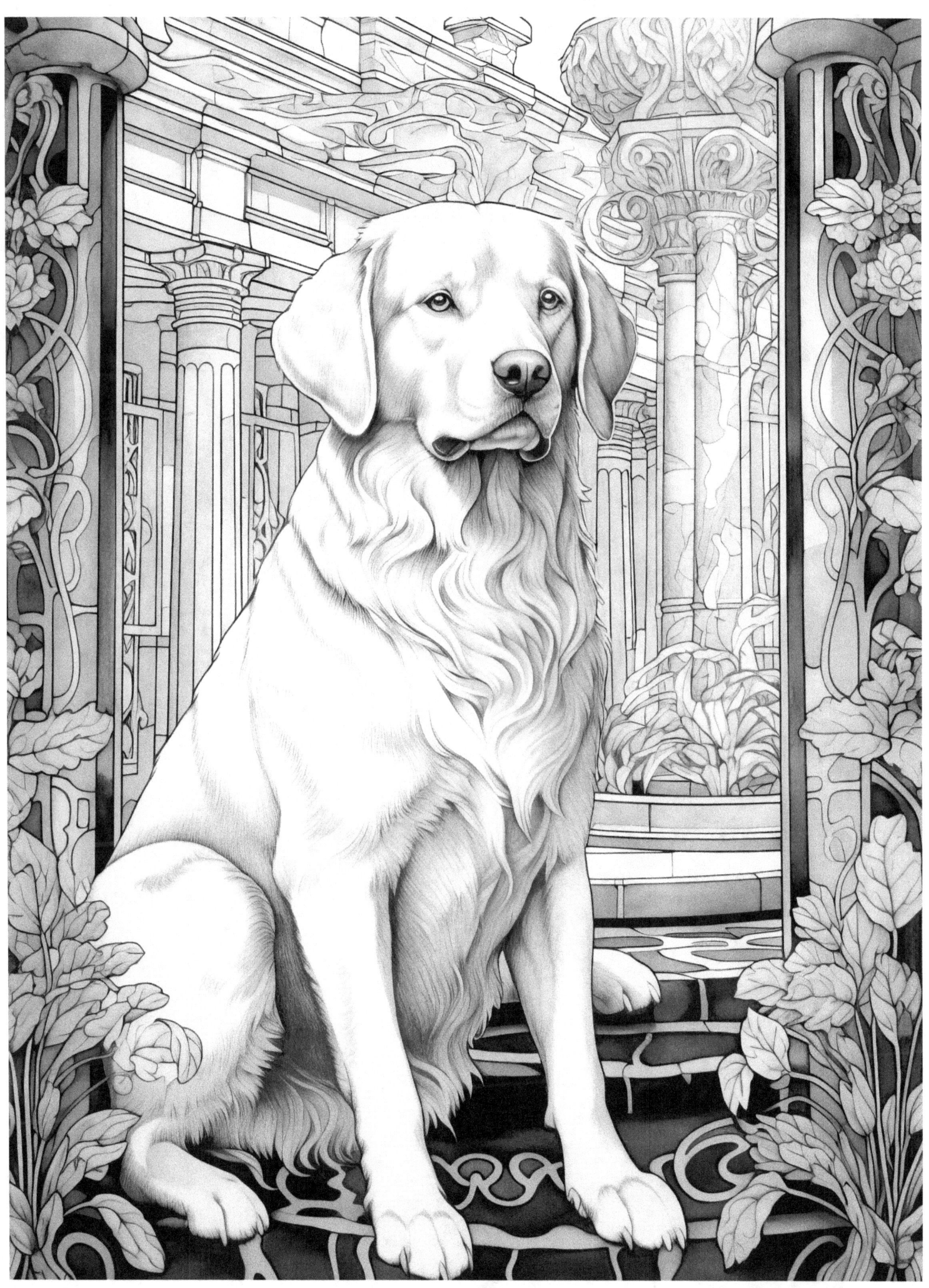

THIS PAGE
INTENTIONALLY
LEFT BLANK.

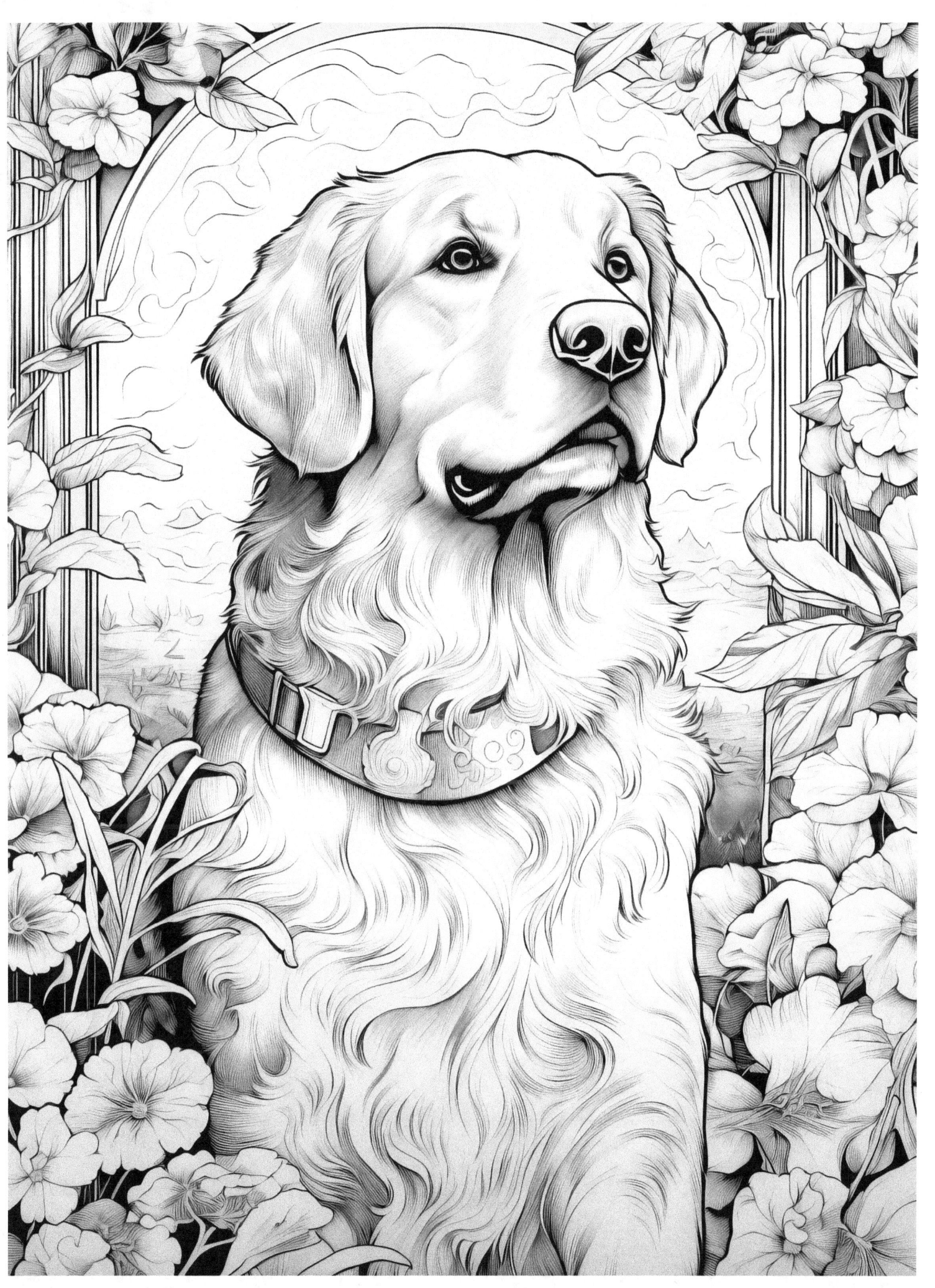

THIS PAGE
INTENTIONALLY
LEFT BLANK.

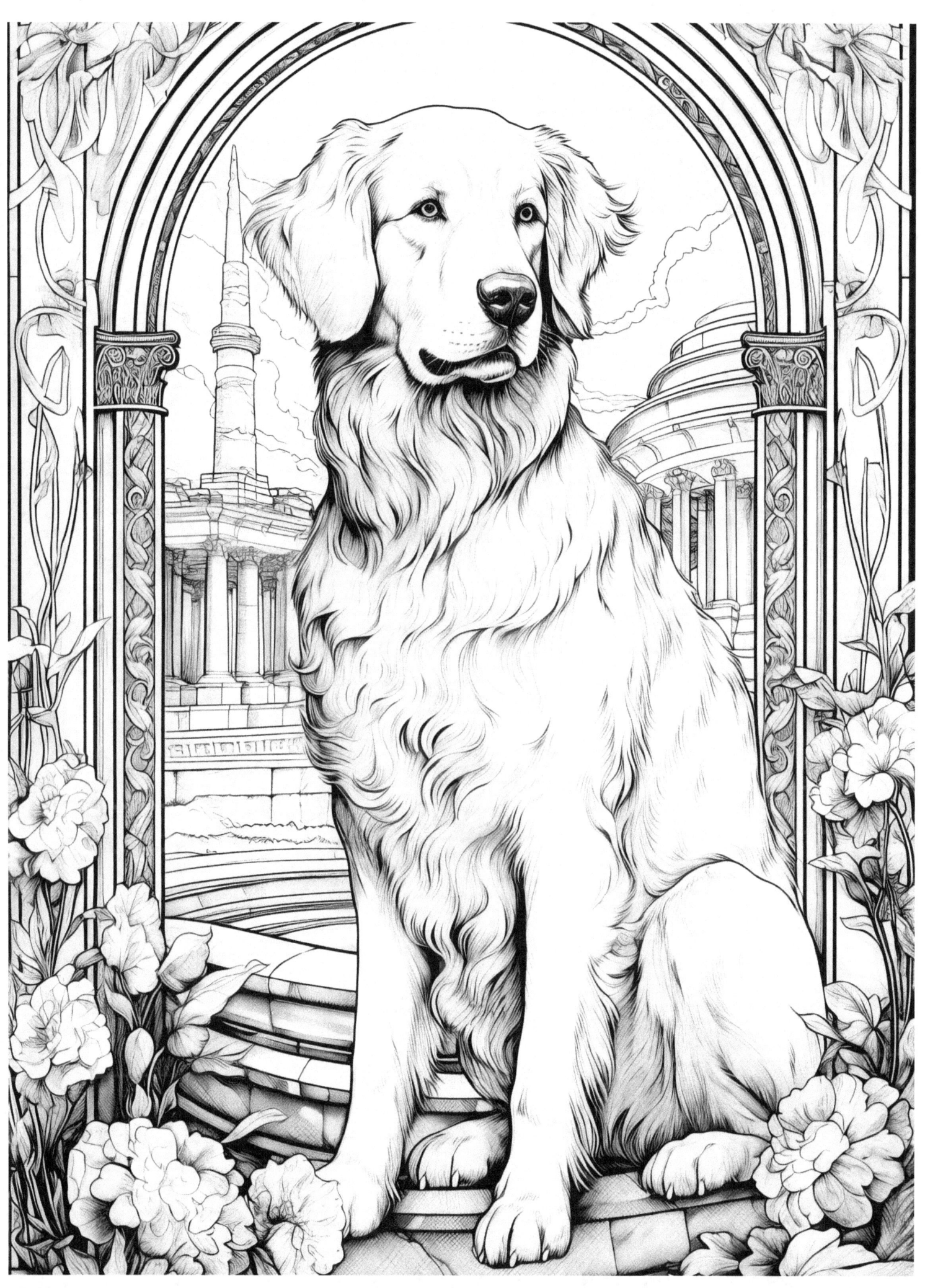

THIS PAGE
INTENTIONALLY
LEFT BLANK.

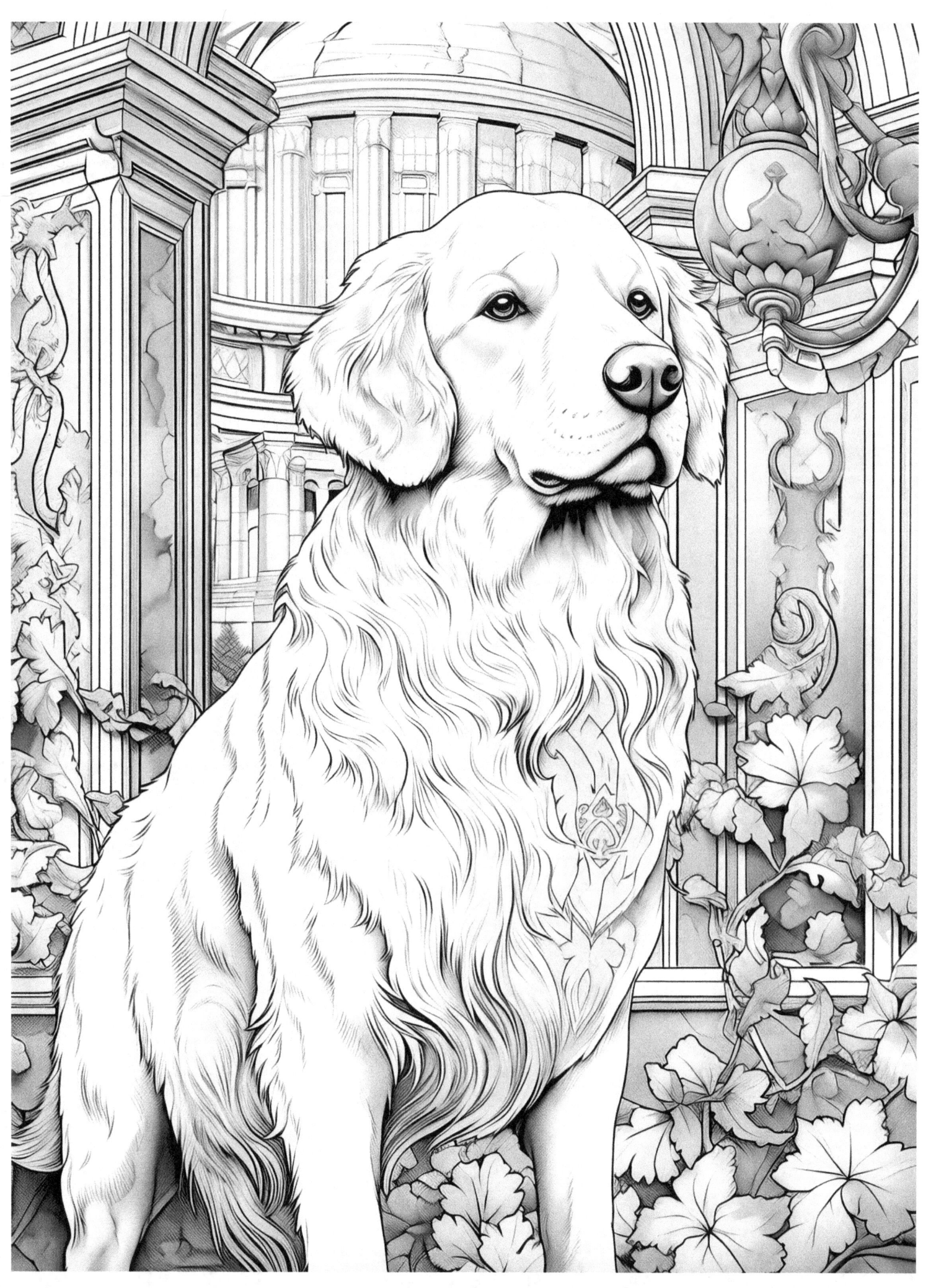

THIS PAGE
INTENTIONALLY
LEFT BLANK.

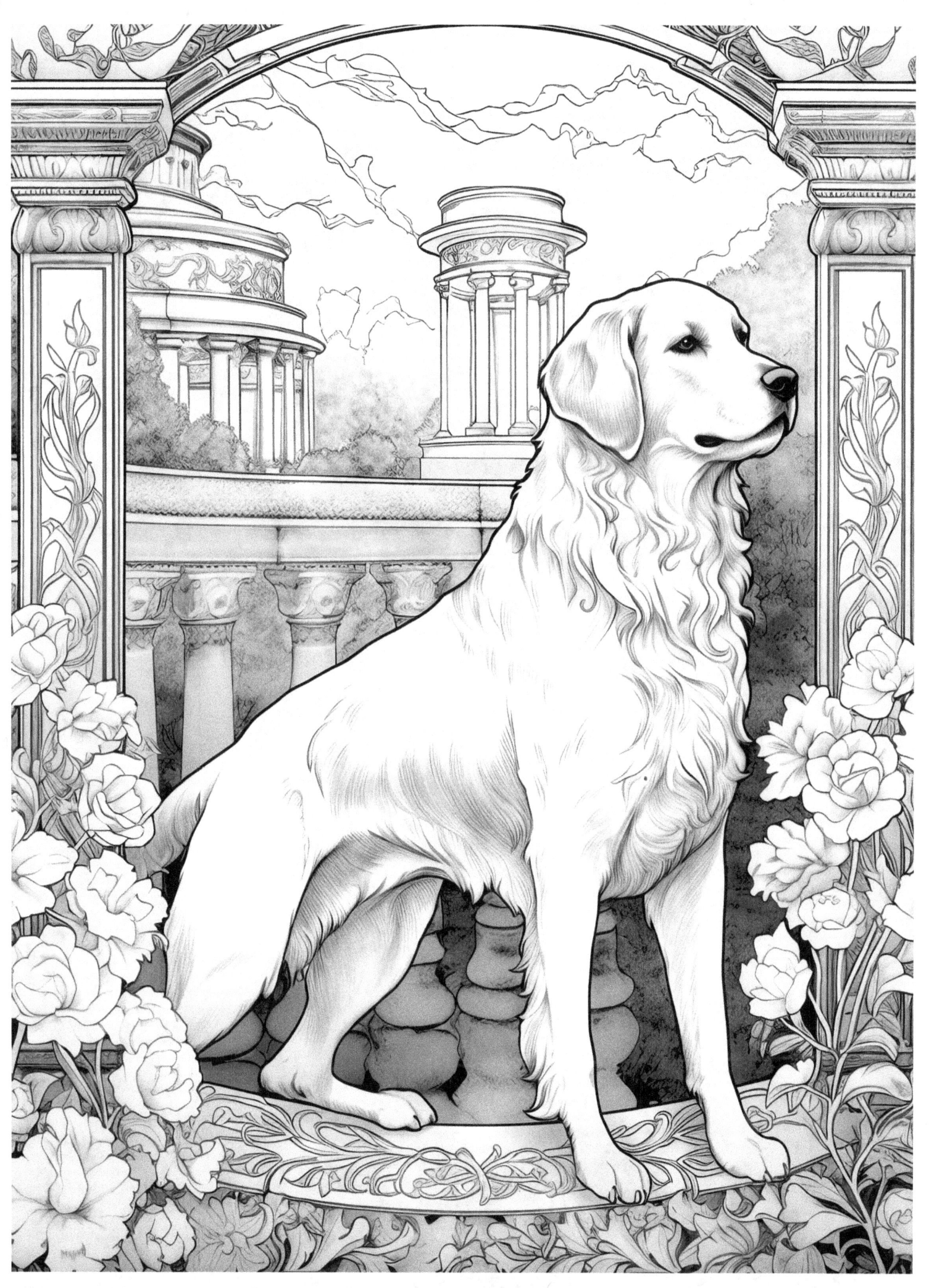

THIS PAGE
INTENTIONALLY
LEFT BLANK.

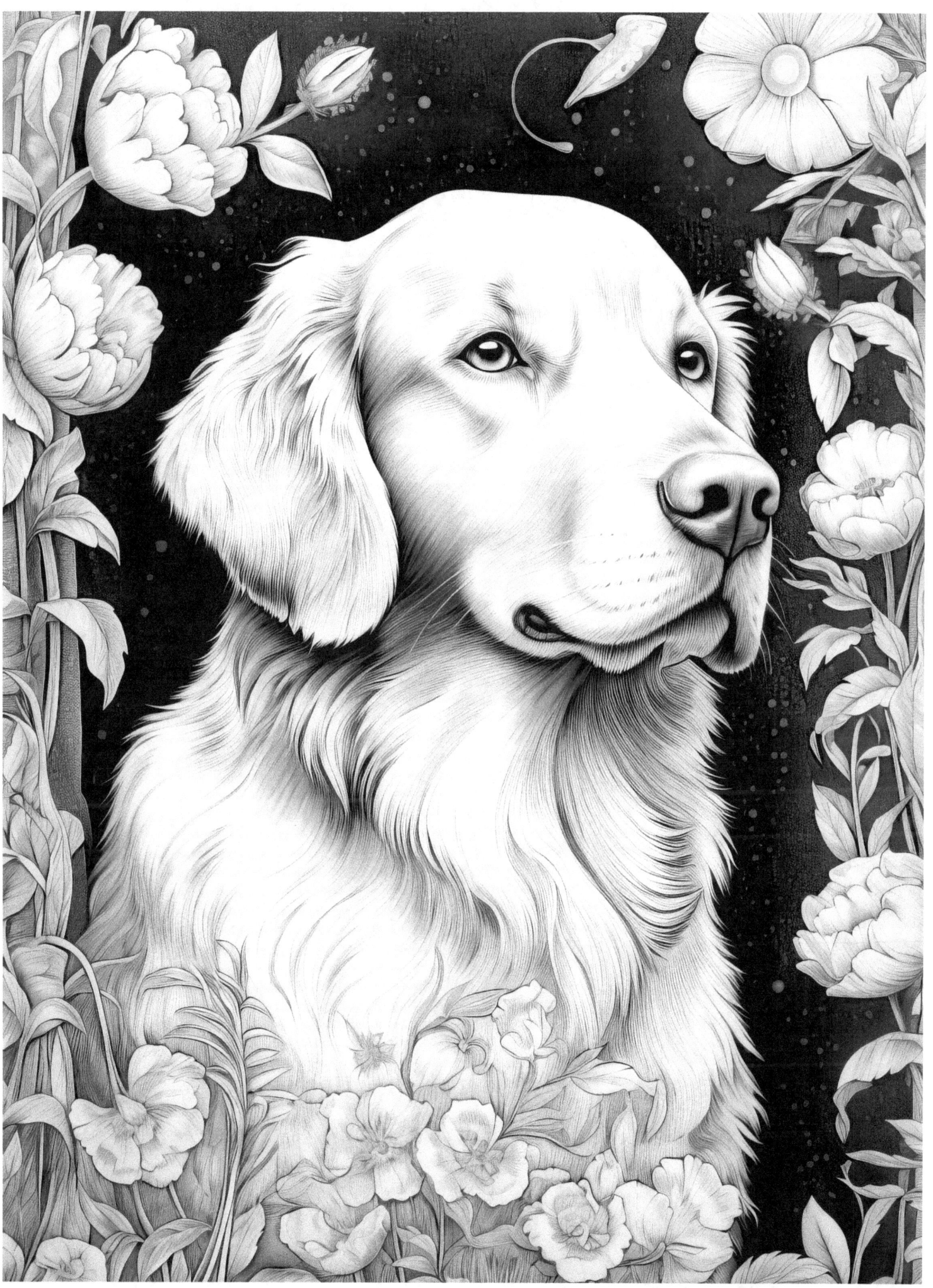

THIS PAGE
INTENTIONALLY
LEFT BLANK.

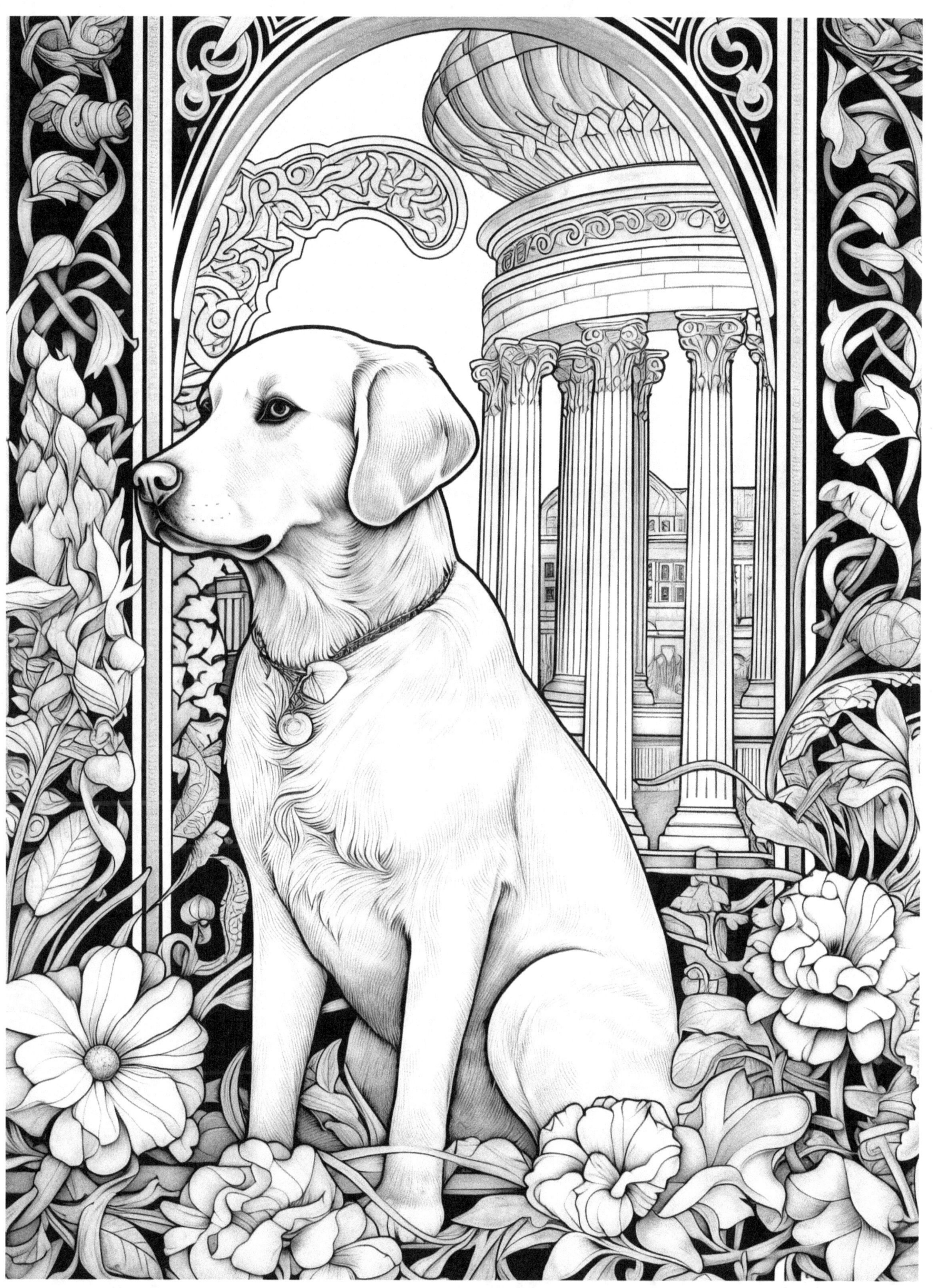

THIS PAGE
INTENTIONALLY
LEFT BLANK.

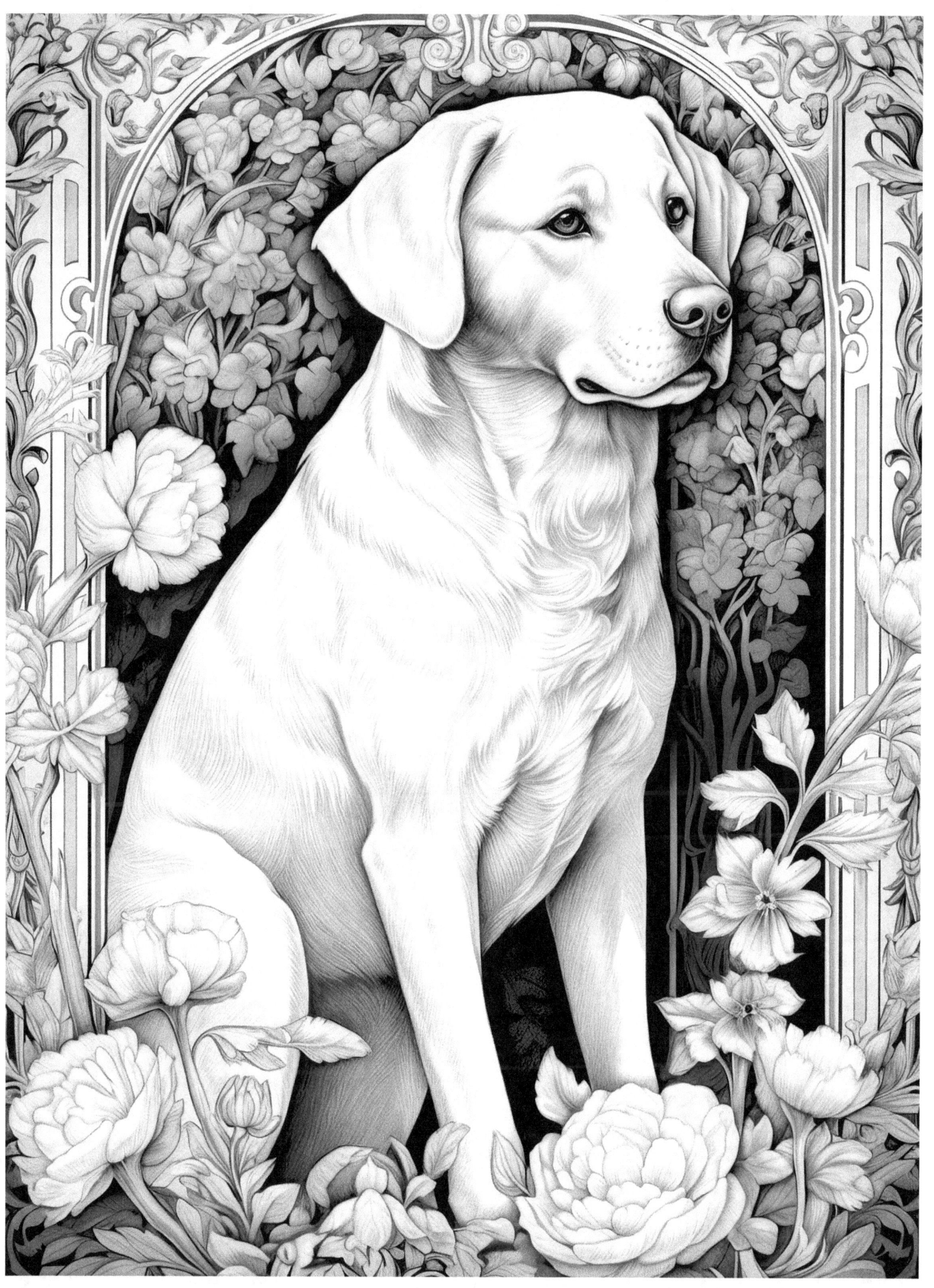

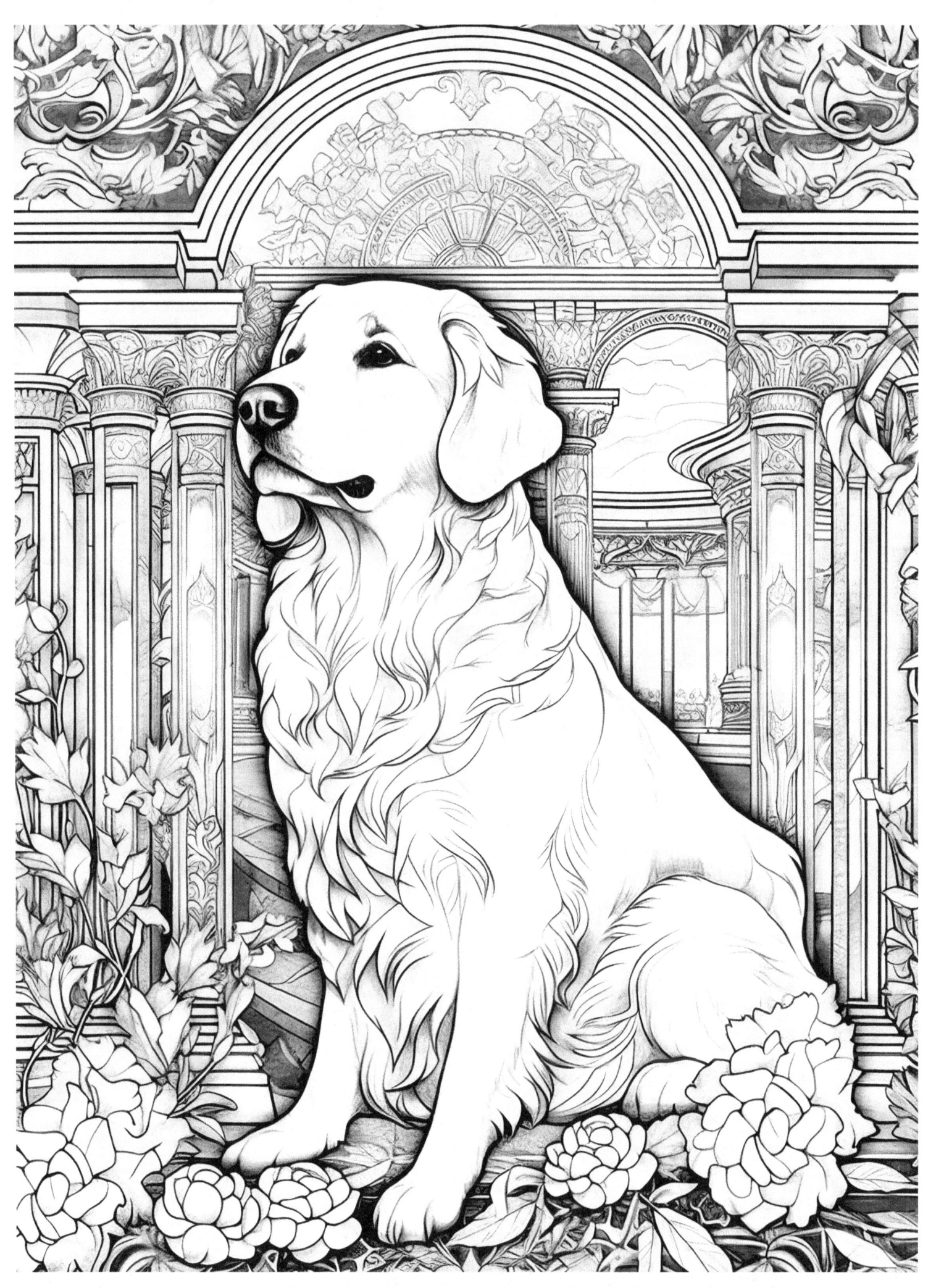

THIS PAGE
INTENTIONALLY
LEFT BLANK.

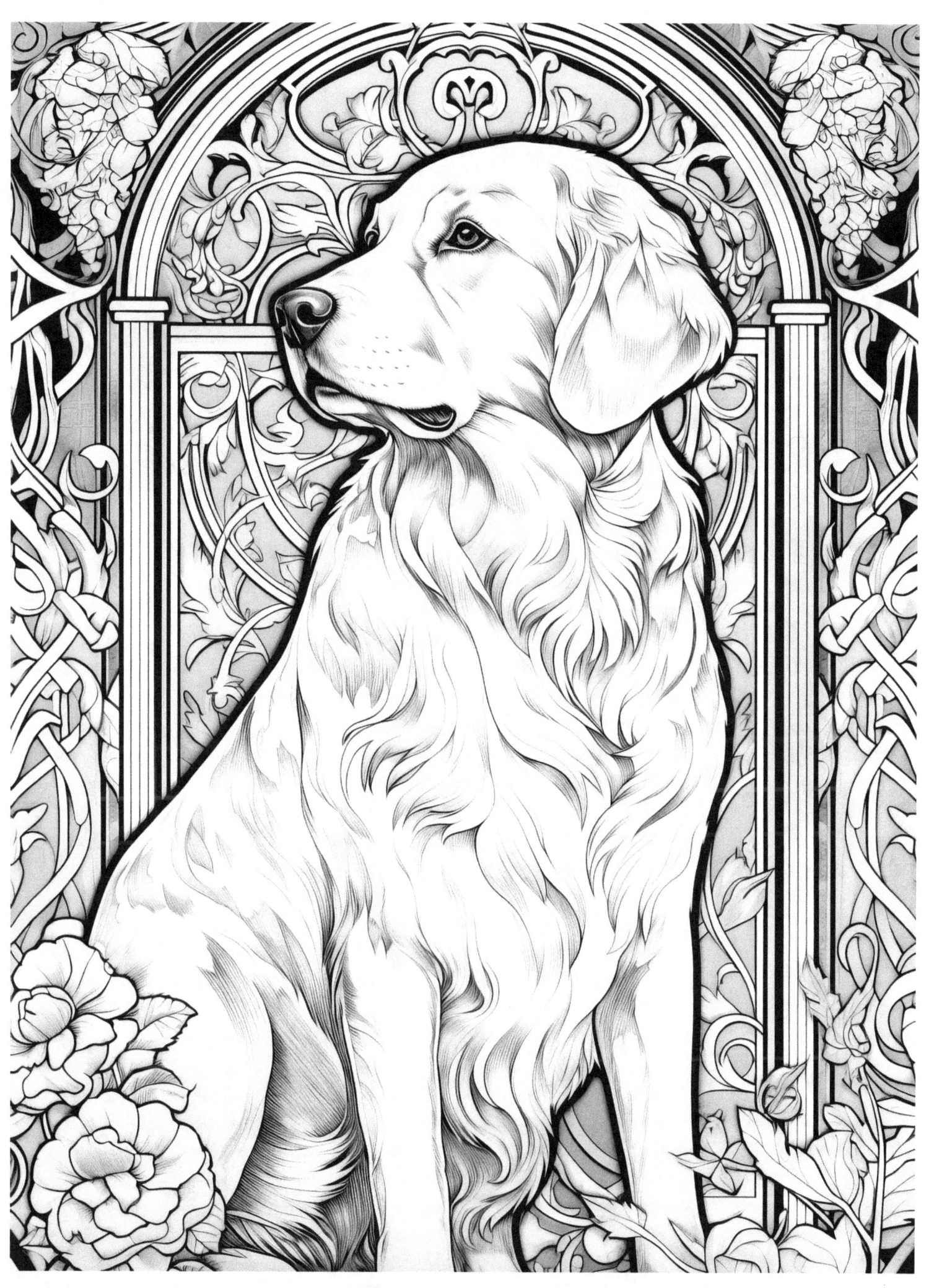

THIS PAGE
INTENTIONALLY
LEFT BLANK.

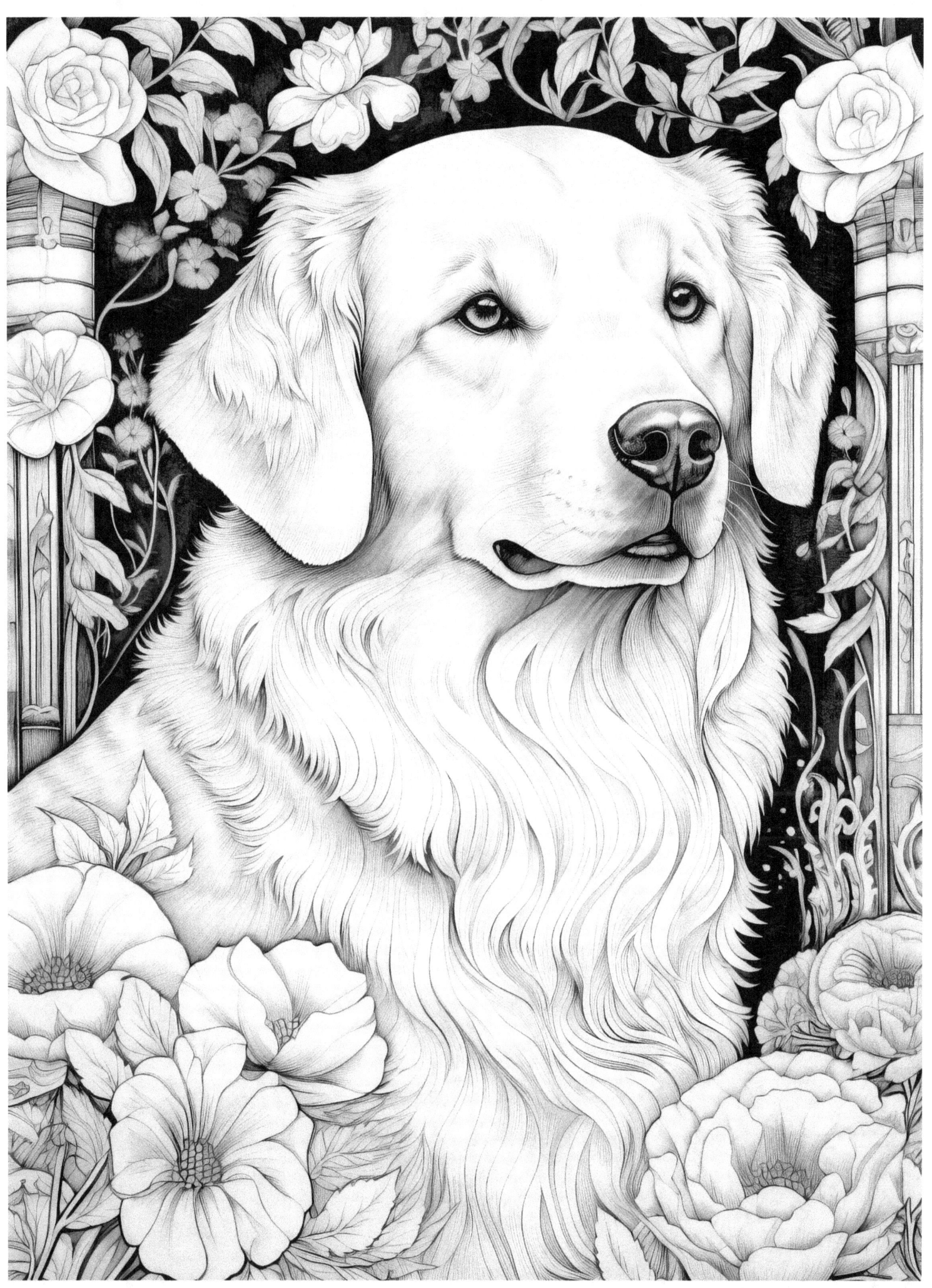

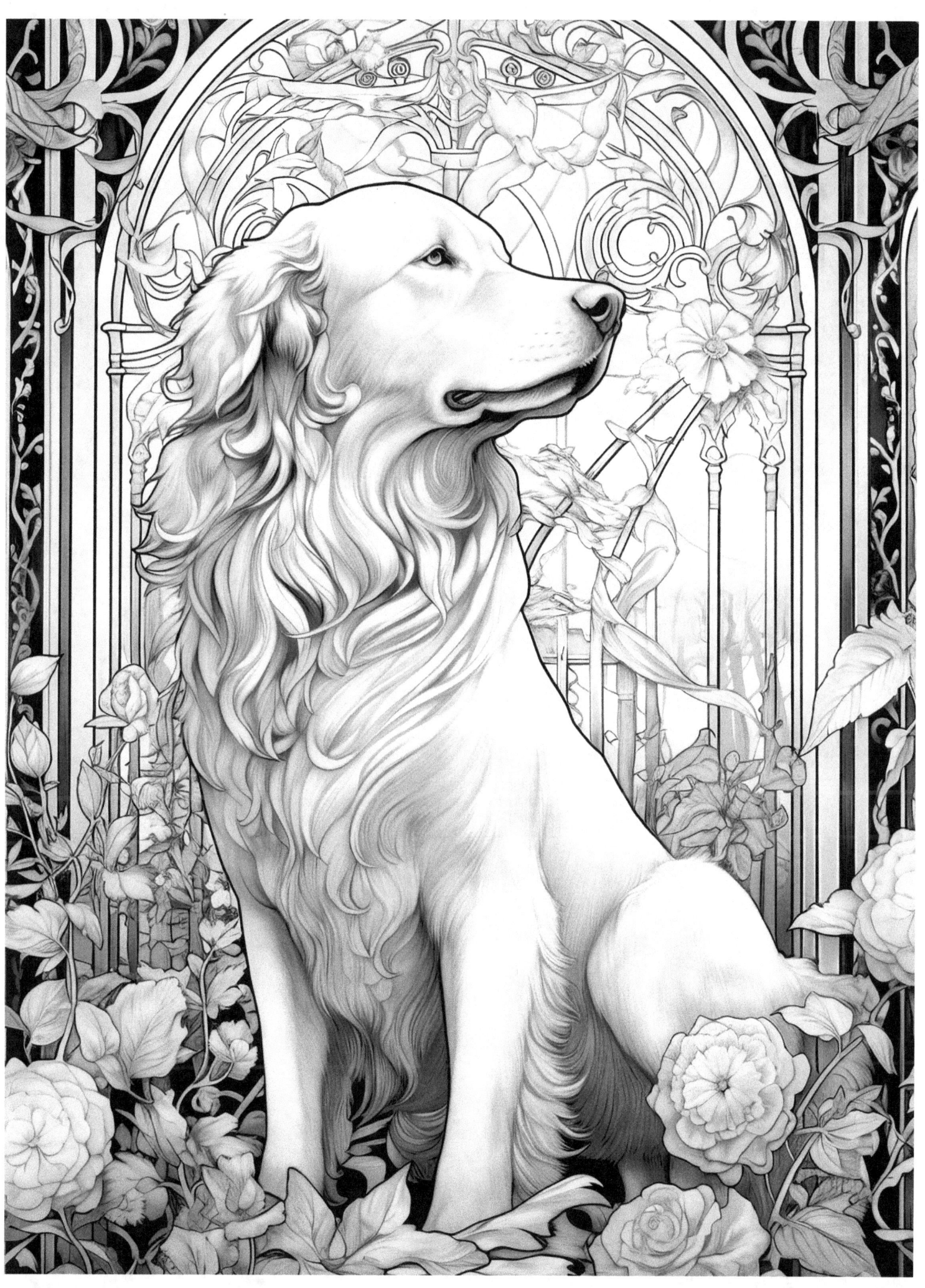

THIS PAGE
INTENTIONALLY
LEFT BLANK.

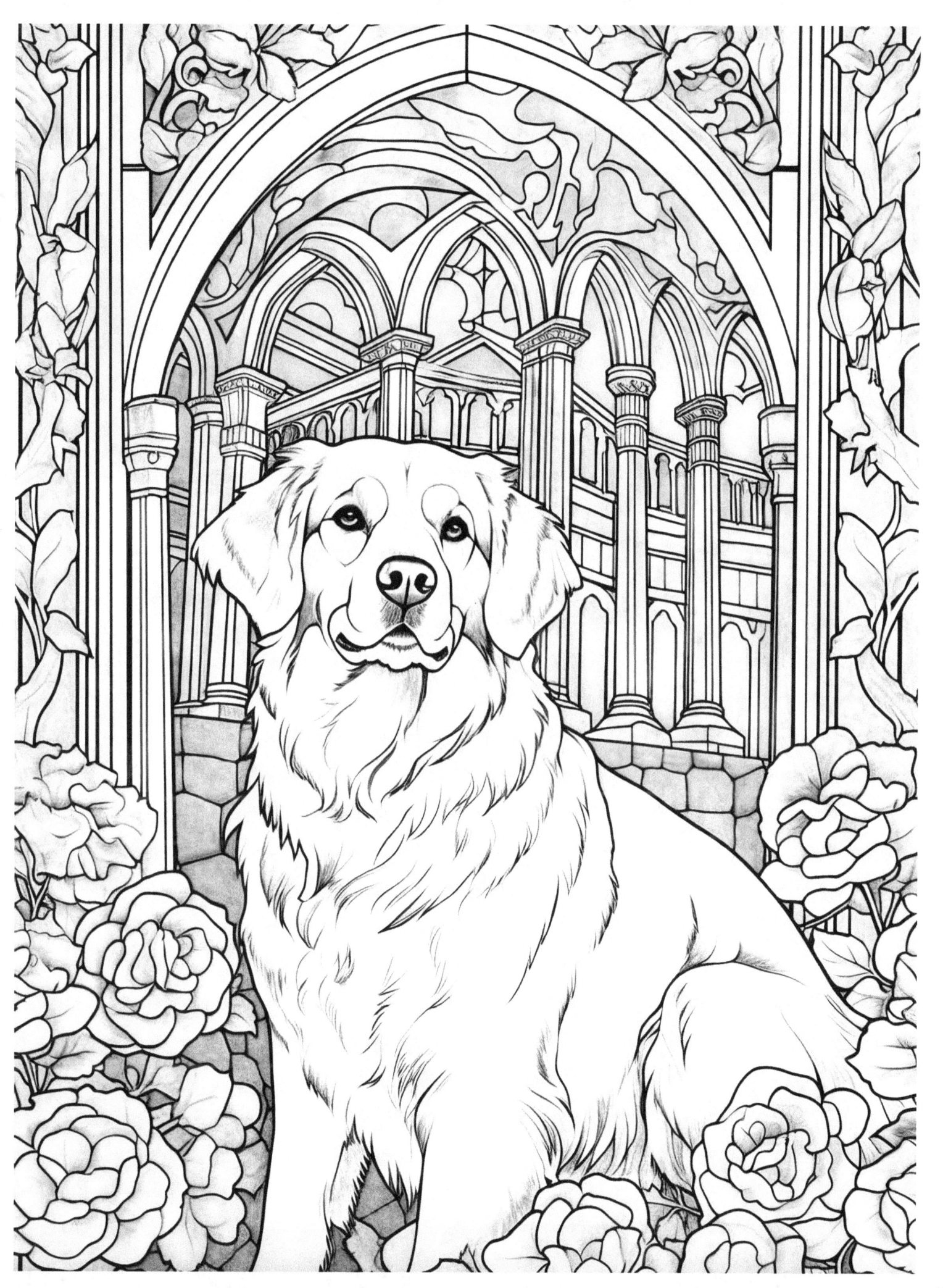

THIS PAGE INTENTIONALLY LEFT BLANK.

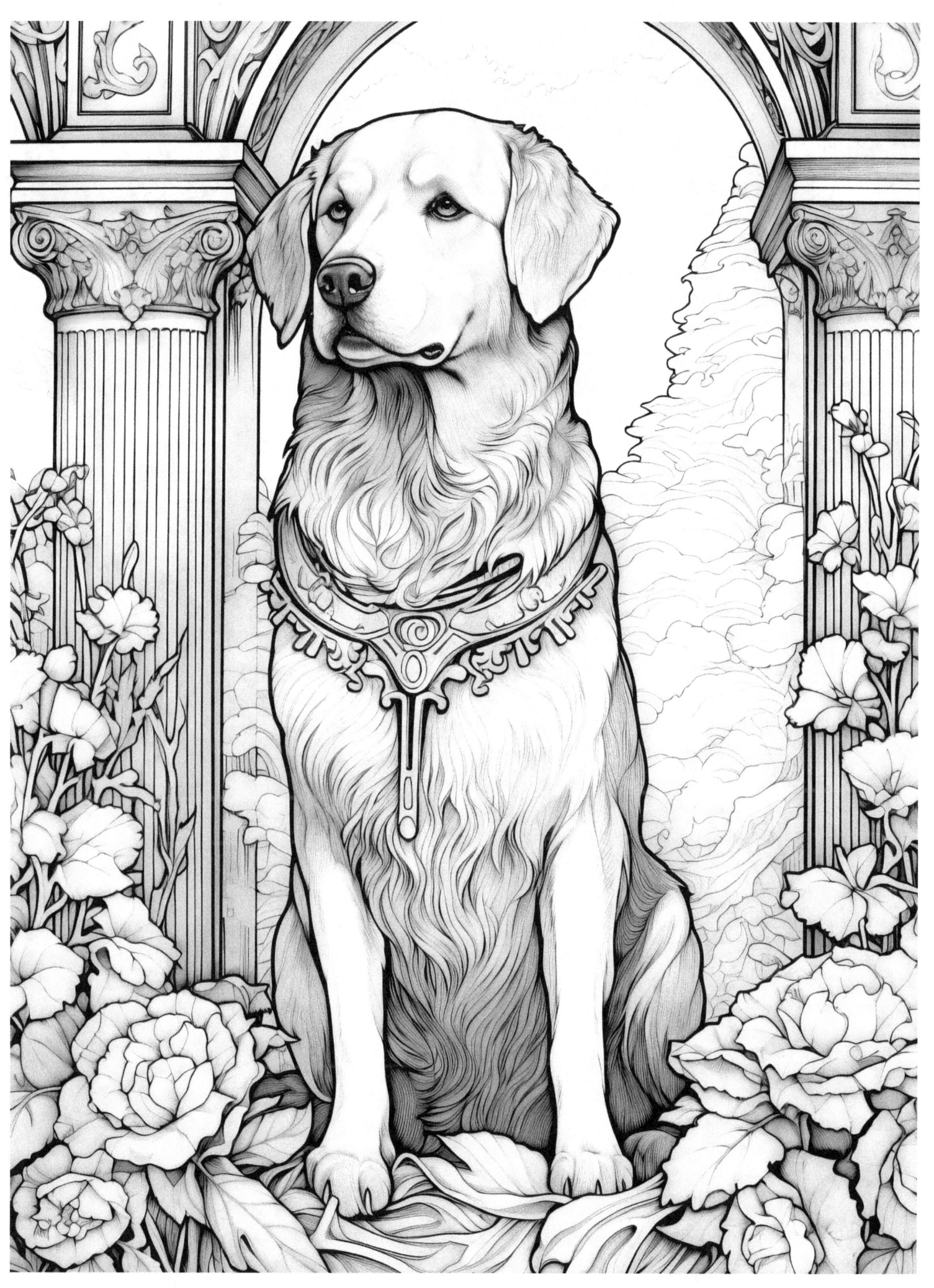

THIS PAGE
INTENTIONALLY
LEFT BLANK.